THEATRE IN REVIEW

D0655814

792.
015
Lum

3 weeks

THEATRE IN REVIEW

ERIC BLOM   ALAN DENT   GERARD FAY
JOHN FERNALD   CHARLES GRAVES
OLAV PAUS GRUNT   ANTHONY HARTLEY
IAIN HAMILTON   PHILIP HOPE-WALLACE
LUDOVIC KENNEDY   JOHN MOODY
YVONNE MITCHELL   ISABEL QUIGLY
MICHEL SAINT-DENIS   JOHN SHAND
——   LOTHIAN SMALL   J. A. WILSON
SANDY WILSON   T. C. WORSLEY   ——

EDITED BY
FREDERICK LUMLEY

RICHARD PATERSON

Richard Paterson Limited, Edinburgh

London Institute
Central Saint Martins College of
Art & Design Library
ACC. No. ..Cl.l.2.a.a.4.60..
DATE ....1.6/7/03.............
CLASS No. ....792.615. LUM
BDG. DATES ....3ush.

Book Centre Catalogue No. Z 800

First published 1956

PRINTED IN GREAT BRITAIN BY
J. AND J. GRAY, EDINBURGH

Withdrawn From
Central Saint Martins
College of Art & Design Library

Contents

		PAGE
Introduction		xiii
THE LONDON STAGE: DRUGS NO ANSWER	*Anthony Hartley*	1
ATMOSPHERE	*Philip Hope-Wallace*	16
The Gardener's Lament (from *Electra*) translated by Lothian Small	*Jean Giraudoux*	21
MUSIC AS DRAMA'S HANDMAID	*Eric Blom*	25
THE FRENCH DRAMATIC CENTRES	*Michel Saint-Denis*	32
The Queen and the Rebels (a scene from the translation by Henry Reed)	*Ugo Betti*	48
THE ACTOR'S POINT OF VIEW	*Yvonne Mitchell*	54
STRATFORD AND SHAKESPEARIAN PRODUCTION	*T. C. Worsley*	61
THE BRISTOL OLD VIC	*John Moody*	69
PLAYGOING OVER HERE AND OVER THERE	*Alan Dent*	74
THE IRISH THEATRE—A DECLINE AND PERHAPS, IN THE END, A FALL	*Gerard Fay*	80
Blood Wedding (two passages from Roy Campbell's translation)	*Garcia Lorca*	90
THE SCOTTISH SCENE	*Charles Graves*	94
NOTES FROM NORWAY	*Olav Paus Grunt*	101
Partage de Midi (a scene translated by Lothian Small)	*Paul Claudel*	106

v

CONTENTS

		PAGE
THOSE WHO CAN'T, CRITICIZE	*Iain Hamilton*	113
FIRST NIGHT	*Ludovic Kennedy*	129
Murder Story (a scene from the play by Ludovic Kennedy)		135
ART THEATRE OR SHOW BUSINESS	*John Fernald*	142
THE CINDERELLA OF THE MUSES	*Lothian Small*	147
TELEVISION AND THE THEATRE	*Isabel Quigly*	160
THE EYES HAVE IT	*J. A. Wilson*	171
It is Midnight, Dr Schweitzer (a scene from Lothian Small's translation)	*Gilbert Cesbron*	178
A FUTURE FOR BRITISH MUSICALS	*Sandy Wilson*	185
MUSIC HALL—THE MEMORY LINGERS ON	*John Shand*	189
Marius (a scene translated by Lothian Small)	*Marcel Pagnol*	196

Illustrations

between pages 40 *and* 41

THE CENTRE DRAMATIQUE DE L'EST, STRASBOURG

Members at rehearsal
A production by Michel Saint-Denis of Jean Anouilh's *La Sauvage*

Michel Saint-Denis' production of *Tessa* by Jean Giraudoux

Michèle Manet and Dominique Bernard in Marivaux's *La Surprise de l'Amour*

A scene from Molière's *Le Misanthrope*
    (*Photographs for above are by* Carabin-C.D.E. and Ville de Colmar)

between pages 64 *and* 65

THE STRATFORD COMPANY

Michael Benthall's production of *The Tempest*, decor by Loudon
Sainthill   (*Photo:* Angus McBean)

The Australian tour of *Othello*, produced by Anthony Quayle, decor by
Tanya Moiseiwitsch   (*Photo:* Angus McBean)

Glen Byam Shaw's production of *Anthony and Cleopatra*. Decor by
Motley. With Peggy Ashcroft as Cleopatra and Marius Goring as
Caesar   (*Photo:* Angus McBean)

All's Well that Ends Well, produced by Noel William, decor by Mariano
Andreu

Glen Byam Shaw's production of *Troilus and Cressida*, decor by Malcolm
Pride   (*Both photos by* Angus McBean)

between pages 112 *and* 113

The Bristol Old Vic's production of *Marching Song*, by John Whiting
                (*Photo:* Desmond Tripp)

Much Ado About Nothing, produced by the Bristol Old Vic
                (*Photo:* Desmond Tripp)

Michael Warre's decor for 'Flint Castle' in Sir Ralph Richardson's Old Vic production of *Richard II*

Tanya Moiseiwitsch's decor for *Henry VIII*   (*Photo:* Angus McBean)

between pages 184 *and* 185

Edgar's costume in *King Lear*, designed by Roger Furse

French dramatic Centre costume, by Abd el Kader Farrah, for Calderon's *Alcade de Zalaméa*

A scene from Sandy Wilson's outstanding success *The Boy Friend*
(*Photo: Picture Post* Library)

The Music Hall in the good old days. Lithograph by Alfred Concanen
(*Photo:* Mander-Mitchenson Theatre Collection)

Acknowledgements

Thanks are due to the following authors, agents and publishers for permission to include passages from plays in this book:

to the executors of Jean Giraudoux, for ' The Gardener's Lament ' from *Electre*, translated by Lothian Small.

Curtis Brown Ltd., for a passage from *The Queen and the Rebels* by Ugo Betti, translated by Henry Reed.

Miss Karin Alin and the executors of Garcia Lorca, for two passages from *Blood Wedding*, translated by Roy Campbell.

Librairie Gallimard, for a passage from *Partage de Midi* by Paul Claudel, translated by Lothian Small. Copyright Librairie Gallimard, tous droits réservés.

M. Gilbert Cesbron and Robert Laffront, éditeur, Paris, for a passage from *Il est Minuit, Dr. Schweitzer*, translated by Lothian Small.

The extract from Marius in the translation of Lothian Small is included by permission of M. Pagnol and Fasquelle, Editeurs.

Contributor's Who's Who

ERIC BLOM is a music critic and editor of the fifth edition of *Grove's Dictionary of Music and Musicians*. Music critic of *The Observer*, 1949–1954. Author of many books on music, including *Everyman's Dictionary of Music*.

ALAN DENT has been dramatic critic of the *News Chronicle* since 1945. London critic of the *Manchester Guardian* 1935–1943, prior to which he was private secretary to the late James Agate.

GERARD FAY is London Editor of the *Manchester Guardian*. He has family connexions with the Abbey Theatre, Dublin, being the son of Frank Fay and nephew of W. G. Fay.

JOHN FERNALD is director of the Royal Academy of Dramatic Arts. He has produced extensively both in West End and arts theatres. Author of *The Play Produced*.

CHARLES GRAVES is dramatic critic of *The Scotsman*.

OLAV PAUS GRUNT has been dramatic critic since 1948 of the Norwegian magazine *Vi Selv og våre hjem*, and is a regular contributor to *Aftenposten*.

IAIN HAMILTON is Associate Editor of the *Spectator* and dramatic critic for the *Times Educational Supplement*.

ANTHONY HARTLEY is dramatic critic of the *Spectator*.

PHILIP HOPE-WALLACE has been London dramatic critic of the *Manchester Guardian* since 1946. He is also dramatic critic of *Time and Tide* and *The Listener*.

LUDOVIC KENNEDY is an author and playwright.

FREDERICK LUMLEY is author of a critical survey of the modern theatre, *Trends in Twentieth Century Drama.*

YVONNE MITCHELL made her first West End appearance in 1944 and has now become a star of stage, screen and TV.

JOHN MOODY is director of the Bristol Old Vic Theatre Company.

ISABEL QUIGLY is film critic of the *Spectator.* Her first novel *The Eyes of Heaven* was recently published.

MICHEL SAINT-DENIS began his career as secretary to Jacques Copeau. In 1930 founded La Compagnie des Quinze and in 1935 founded London Theatre Studio. Appointed director of the Old Vic in 1950, he is now director of the Centre dramatique de l'Est.

JOHN SHAND (died 1955) was on the London editorial staff of the *Manchester Guardian.* He had family connexions with the music hall stage.

LOTHIAN SMALL has translated a good round dozen French plays, including Anouilh, Cesbron, Cocteau and Vildrac, and a few modern German and Italian playwrights.

J. A. WILSON was formerly film critic of *The Scotsman.* Is now working in B.B.C. Television.

SANDY WILSON has written the most successful of modern British musicals, *The Boy Friend.* His latest success is *The Buccaneer.*

T. C. WORSLEY is dramatic critic of *The New Statesman and Nation,* and author of *The Fugitive Art.*

Introduction

looking forward and back

A S LATE AS 1923 it was still possible for William Archer
to refer to *The Old Drama and the New*, thankful that the
former had been swept away by the sharp northerly air let
into the fusty drawing-room of Victorian memory. The
metamorphosis had been completed, a surrender made to a
theatre which was actual and natural—the future seemed as
bright as bright could be. Yet the theatre, like the 'brave
new world', soon was to become neither so brave nor so
new. Struggling through a succession of crises, and faced
with the rise of the film as an art and in the last decade
television as a craft, the theatre was clearly on trial for its
life. Words such as 'old' and 'new' have lost their
meaning, only a great fear hangs over the stage today like
the sword of Damocles. Unperturbed our theatrical
entrepreneurs stand by and seem to do nothing while we
all watch with morbid curiosity, quite powerless as the
lights go out one by one in the theatres all over the country.

Theatre in Review has grown and been built up against this
background. If all had been well in the theatre a book of
this nature might have easily contented itself with recaptur-
ing the memories of a thousand and one nights full of
nostalgic interest for theatre-lovers, as its readers might like
to pass an hour, not upon the stage, but in the company of
old theatre programmes. In short we might have presented
a kind of bedside book, into which our readers could have
dipped as into a treasure chest. But alas, all is not well in

the theatre and this original idea had from the start to be abandoned. In its place we have assembled a collection of essays which discuss the vital problems and contribute a lively and controversial general survey on the state of the theatre. Controversial, for critics of course always beg to differ, and it has been our intention here to encourage frank and direct speaking. Our authors can certainly be relied on for stimulating discussion, but whatever their differences in outlook they are united by a common love of the theatre. However alarmed they may be at the low ebb serious theatre has reached, they accept the crisis neither as a *fait accompli* nor dismiss it with foolhardy optimism. While recognizing that the theatre may be mortal, we can take heart remembering that this is not the first time it has been a sick man; and in these essays ground for hope may be found in the life that there still is today which could well assert itself everywhere if only it were given the chance.

One of the most promising experiments, which Michel Saint-Denis describes, is that of the various French Dramatic Centres. Since leaving the Old Vic, M. Saint-Denis has been director of the Eastern Centre, based on Strasbourg. The French Centres have succeeded in bringing a repertory of classical and the best of modern plays to audiences who had never known what a straight play was. 'Who would have thought that Shakespeare, Molière and Lorca would be bigger box-office', M. Saint-Denis asks, 'than the dreary hacks of the commercial theatre? And yet that is what has happened'. Surely this is proof of what can be done elsewhere if we have faith in the living drama. The Centres do receive subsidies both from the French Government and from local municipalities, and indeed the theatre in France (which apart from the Centres means the theatre in Paris) has always been fortunate in being divided, like Caesar's Gaul, into three parts, that of the *avant-garde* theatre, that of the subsidized theatres, and finally the *théâtre des boulevards*. In Britain, on the other hand, the theatre is regarded as a commercial proposition, and the rule of the box-office has long been synonymous with success. The conflict, as John Fernald draws the distinction, is between this 'theatre of show business' and 'the theatre of truth', and unfortunately it is only the manifestations of show business that most managements seem to understand. It is true that Britain has in the past been fortunate in discovering outstanding men who have come to the front on their own initiative, but the economics of high finance in the theatre together with the gradual squeeze of entrepreneurs makes the success or even appearance of a Cochrane today more and more unlikely, and thus hopes of the showman as dedicated theatre artist fades. The public is left with only what the showmen of today offer, and they, playing safe, in place of creating values and taste follow the common denominator. It is a sorry vacuum, but is it not responsible for the turning of audiences away from the theatre towards mediums which serve them better? When will the theatre managements realize that the theatre, if it is to continue its living traditions, must lead, not follow? Fortunately the situation demands challenge, and it is in this spirit that our contributors present the case for the theatre. The theatre will only die if theatre-goers accept the fact.

To remind ourselves that the modern theatre is not devoid of good plays we have selected short passages from some half a dozen which have achieved international reputation. That so few worth-while plays are British is not difficult to understand, in the light of Mr Kennedy's article, and in view of the treatment a young writer may expect from the hands of theatre powers, Mr Hartley's remark that few writers of talent today any longer 'consider writing for the stage' is an answer to the question, 'where are the good plays?'

This book requires not an introduction, but an epilogue, a kind of judge's summing-up. That we shall leave to you, dear reader, to continue the discussion far into the night. All the writing, talking, indeed all the king's men will not cure the patient; but if this book has done some service in

making clear the dangers and dispelling complacency, if
as a result the patient begins to sit up, then it will have
fulfilled its purpose. We must remember that the theatre,
like life, is capable of the miraculous. After all showmen
declare that there's no business like show business. It can
also behave like a fickle child and let you down. Was it
not Beaumarchais who likened plays to children, 'conceived
with pleasure, carried about before they are born with great
fatigue, and brought forth in pain; scarcely ever do they
recompense their parents, and they cost more sorrow than
they give delight'? If sometimes we despair and ask whether
the theatre really is worth while, the answer must surely be
that the theatre, after all, is human. Which means YES.

F. L.

The London Stage:
Drugs no Answer

*

by *Anthony Hartley*

FIRST a few definitions. Let it be understood that I am
talking throughout this essay about serious theatre,
and that by this I mean serious theatre in the West End, as
well as such peripheral experimental and club theatres as
create a style or a fashion before it becomes sufficiently
popular to bear bringing to the commercial stage. Of course
it may be objected that it is artificial and even priggish to
treat serious theatre in isolation. So long as audiences turn
up in their thousands to see the latest equivalent of *Worm's
Eye View* or (very sensibly) to laugh at the Crazy Gang,
why worry? Is not this a sign that theatre is holding its
own against TV and the cinema? However, I believe that
anyone who cares for theatre must insist upon the setting
of an ideal far beyond a deserving West End success.
Separate Tables is an excellent straight play in its way, but
it should surely be apparent that a theatre which chooses
Mr Rattigan for its ideal is doomed to extinction or, at all
events, to sink into that sub-cultural region which the
English stage occupied throughout a large part of the
eighteenth and nineteenth centuries. A serious play is a
play that lasts, and a play that lasts is a play that bears reading
afterwards. This is a very simple truth which a moment's
thought about the history of world drama suffices to discover, but it does seem in some danger of being forgotten.
How many plays can stand printing these days? The words
'good theatre' all too often sound like a knell over the grave

of serious drama, indicating, as they do, the sacrifice of the playwright to producer and actors. It is, in fact, difficult to avoid the impression that the English theatre is dying at the top. And we all know what happens to trees that do that. But let us look a little more closely at the situation.

*   *   *

Anyone under the age of thirty must, I think, be increasingly conscious of a disaffection towards the theatre spreading among his contemporaries. This has so far been masked by the fact that, being felt among the younger generation, it has not as yet had much influence on box-office money, but it will soon begin to make itself noticed. A friend of mine, who is a university lecturer, recently remarked to me that he never went to the theatre, which he considered a most unrewarding experience, and the seriousness of a situation in which such a remark can be made should not be concealed by the fact that the Old Vic can always be filled with school children or that people still take their girls to musicals.

Compare this state of affairs with what is happening in the cinema world. For the serious film there is in this country a genuinely popular audience (i.e. an audience composed of intelligent people drawn from all walks of life), as anyone who cares to go to the National Film Theatre on the South Bank can see for himself. Now, the cinema by its collective nature is a medium in which it is far easier to produce entirely commercialized trash than in the theatre. For one thing, there is a greater temptation to do so, given the mass audiences for which it caters. Under these circumstances it is surely a reproach to the world of the theatre that it has lost this same intelligent audience that exists for films. Admittedly the cinema can draw its films from every country in the world, but the stage, which, after all, can always put on foreign plays, comes off badly even if due allowance is made for this. The people who are prepared to queue on the South Bank could and should be going to the theatre. To ask why they are not is the first question that should be posed about the English stage today.

Partly, I suppose, it has to do with the *chi-chi* surrounding the theatre: the donning of lounge suits, the not very convenient times of the curtain and so forth do discourage people who might otherwise go. So incidentally does the high price of theatre tickets. And here the managements have been very foolish (as compared with their fellows in other countries) in not putting forward a large-scale scheme for cheaper tickets for students and other young people. By so doing they would have built up an appreciative and critical audience, which would have acquired the habit of theatre-going young. Of course, if they do not want such an audience—and a really critical audience might prove a little awkward for some of these entrepreneurs—it is quite understandable that they should do nothing about encouraging it. But they ought to be clear about one thing: the alternative to a critical audience is no audience at all.

Another point is more delicate and can only be made with some reservations. A good deal has recently been talked about a certain state of mind and approach to life common to a number of young writers. This approach is, broadly speaking, a continuation of the English nonconformist tradition and includes such characteristics as hostility to æstheticism, sturdily egalitarian feeling and a hatred of shams, which extends to many forms of conventional manners. Now, it is difficult to say how far this attitude is representative of that of the educated public between the ages of twenty and thirty-five today. I believe it to be representative of a fairly large section of them—in particular of the growing class of technicians turned out by provincial universities. However this may be, it seems to be a fact that there is, in this particular manifestation of the *zeitgeist*, a fundamental hostility, not merely to plays put on at the moment, but also to the contemporary world of the theatre as such. It is hard to be definite about this, but one can see how the curious lack of modernity about the London stage, a sort of attitude artificially maintained from before the first World War, might estrange this fraction of the public. Even taken in itself the cinema is more modern than the theatre, where techniques have been almost at a standstill for so long now. And, however important or unimportant this young educated public may be quantitatively, there is no doubt that qualitatively their loss of interest in the stage is a serious matter. For it is only from people like them that playwrights can be recruited.

*   *   *

And here we come to what is probably the gravest problem of all those affecting the theatre to-day. Not merely is there a loss of an intelligent public; there is also— and the one is, of course, partly the cause of the other— a loss of intelligent young writers for the stage. I know a number of writers just under or over the age of thirty, and I hardly know one of them who would consider writing a play. If you asked them why I suspect they might answer that, form for form, they preferred to undertake work that was not liable to be emasculated by the censorship of the Lord Chamberlain, or submitted to the self-consciously stagey tricks of producers or the caprices of actors. Managers, producers and actors (not to speak of the egregious Lord Chamberlain) seem to have combined to make the young writer of ideas feel that it is too much bother to try to express them in this medium. Why not write a novel and have done with it? The result is that in a recent competition for a new play practically none of the entries were by people with any obvious gift for writing at all—let alone for writing plays. It is significant that well-known novelists like Charles Morgan and Graham Greene should take up play-writing at a later stage in their careers, when they already possess sufficient authority and influence to get their works put on without fuss.

In this matter much of the onus must rest on the theatre itself. The question of censorship is illuminating in this respect. Quite apart from the fact that the censorship of plays by administrative decision is an attack on free speech, the way in which that censorship is applied (i.e. by the banning of whole fields of discussion) is both illogical and prejudicial to serious drama. To take one instance: at the same time as the Lord Chamberlain was refusing a licence to an adaptation of Gide's *Immoralist* (which turned out to be a bad play, but that has nothing to do with it), a West End musical was showing us girls having their knickers torn off in an apache dance, a spectacle which, however enjoyable in itself, would, one might have thought, have displeased the censor. But no; it is serious discussion of sex that is subversive of public morality, not mere titillation. A more serious incident was the cutting of a review sketch, in which Sir Anthony Eden (while still Foreign Secretary) was made to reflect upon the theme 'always the bridesmaid, but never the bride'. This censorship of satire on members of a government carried out under the auspices of an official of the Crown is surely very objectionable indeed. Would the Lord Chamberlain, one wonders, have been so considerate of the feelings of a member of the Opposition? But I think I have said enough to show both how arbitrary and archaic the censorship is. The point is fairly generally admitted, but yet there has been no concerted move to change the law comparable to that which is being made at the moment by publishers and authors to get the obscenity laws altered. The reason is said to be that theatre managements find it more comfortable to shelter behind the Lord Chamberlain, thus avoiding any risk of prosecution, and, if this is true, their unwillingness to take responsibilities that editors of newspapers and publishers take every day hardly reflects much credit on them. A refusal to fight for freedom of speech on the stage is not the way to encourage young writers to give of their best in this medium, particularly when certain topics are completely barred to them.

Of course there is no easy remedy for the present lack of young playwrights. No doubt writers should be prepared to learn dramatic techniques, to attend rehearsals, to sweat it out in argument with producer and actors. But, quite apart from the fact that they have not usually the time (generally they are doing jobs of one kind or another), the main objection remains. Given the fact that they are willing to try various forms of expression, why should they choose one that puts such obstacles in the way of the novice? One step towards a remedy would be a greater respect for the work of their partner, the playwright, on the part of those engaged in staging a play. The writer, after all, is not a mere provider of raw material for the stage. What he lacks in experience and technique could be supplied by an intelligent and sympathetic producer who would create his playwrights much as a publisher creates his authors or (a better analogy) as an editor creates his contributors. But, whatever the remedy may be, the fact is there: the serious theatre is not being furnished with plays from young or even middle-aged writers who have new ideas to sell.

*   *   *

It seems fairly certain that this fact has something to do with the present alienation of a section of the public from the theatre. One of the evils resulting from it is the appearance of a type of writer, who, because he writes for the theatre, implicitly claims to be excused from too severe a comparison with mere literary standards. Christopher Fry, for example, writes verse drama which has been highly praised, but none of those best qualified to judge would consider him seriously as a poet (see Marius Bewley's notice of *Venus Observed* in *Scrutiny*, where the comparison of Mr Fry with Marlowe is examined by someone who really has some idea of what verse structure means). The theatre, in fact, gets the second-best in writing as well as in thought (compare Mr Morgan's *The Burning Glass* with even the most paradoxical play by Shaw), and that this should be so is coming to be taken for granted by many of the people concerned with it. Where it is not taken for granted there is a natural tendency on the part of managements to import French and American plays—because they are better and because their commercial success has already been tested elsewhere.

In the absence of good serious plays other inducements have to be offered to the audience. As is usual in any art form, the lack of guiding ideas leads to preciosity. If you cannot see a play that will make you think or feel, you can see a set that will be a monument to gracious living or costumes designed after some fifteenth century manuscript that nobody has thought of before. This kind of thing is intended to be clever (like producers' tricks with Shakespeare), but it is really a substitute for living thought, and a development of the parts at the expense of the whole. Eric Bentley in his book *In Search of Theater* has spoken of 'the current school of rococo effeminacy represented in different ways by a host of artists. (To the name of Fry one can add that of Anouilh, or those of designers like Cecil Beaton and the late Christian Berard. The name of actors of this school is legion.)' Indeed, a little consideration will show how deeply the English theatre has been bitten by this particular bug. How often do we see a set that is architecture and not interior decoration? How often do we hear Shakespearian verse spoken strongly and simply? Moreover, this fashion of preciosity has an unfortunate tendency to affect the one or two writers for the stage who might in a better atmosphere produce good plays. We had a recent example of this in John Whiting's play *Marching Song*. In this play there is an excellent fundamental situation: the Chancellor of a defeated country is faced by the necessity of bringing to trial a general who has just returned from a prisoner-of-war camp. For the sake of national unity he does not wish to do this; he therefore asks the general to commit suicide. The general, who in some way that is not clear has suffered a spiritual transformation after a massacre of children perpetrated on his orders by his troops, consents, only to recover his will to live under the influence of an existentialist girl in black slacks. He eventually kills himself as a consequence of what seems to be a sudden realization of the non-platonic nature of passion. The play has two themes: the clash of the individual and *raison d'état* and the nature of passion, which are connected in the person of the general but in no other way, and the presentation of the characters varies between symbolism and straight characterization which the author never quite manages to make coincide. There is an attempt to make the play exist on two different levels (corresponding to the two different themes), which seems to me to become snarled up through mere lack of logic and to end in a cloudy mysticism that has no relation to reality in any sense of the word. Mr Whiting has thrown away his original dramatic impulse in favour of a decorative conception of plot that I should call preciosity. What is irritating about this is that it is all so unnecessary. Tragedy, after all, should appear as the quintessence of the human situation, and for this what is required is a firm grip of concrete detail. Given his situation, all Mr Whiting had to do was to follow his nose and work it out. But that he apparently found impossible.

*   *   *

The English stage then is involved in a vicious circle. The lack of plays with something to say produces preciosity of style, and this, in turn, affects those few plays which are turned out by British playwrights. No doubt this situation is made worse by the consonance of the resulting theatre with the desire to escape from reality which has haunted the British upper and middle classes ever since the war and which can be seen in such widely different phenomena as current religious revivals and the vogue for genteel travel books. Moreover the evil has been magnified by present-day mechanisms of cultural diffusion. The existence of organizations like the Arts Council and of managements like H. M. Tennant Ltd means that a very few people have a very large say in what goes on on the London stage. Of course theatrical combines have always existed, but the present economic situation with its rising costs makes it very hard—harder than ever before—to stage plays without their backing. On the other hand, immediately a fashion has clicked with the mysterious powers that preside over them, it is spread with great rapidity, and anyone who wants to change it will have a great deal of political manœuvring to do in order to succeed—when, of course, he will become fashionable in turn.

*   *   *

What then is to be done with the London theatre? The way out of the vicious circle is obviously through the writer, but, if the writing of more, better and more serious plays is to provide a solution, we must make certain that they *are* better plays. We must not be so entranced with the mere idea of anyone writing drama at all that we see a new Marlowe in every poetaster and a new Ibsen in every writer of so-called 'problem' plays. What, I take it, we must avoid at all costs is the mystical semi-symbolic slush which is churned out when a playwright wants to be 'poetic' so that nowadays the very mention of that misused adjective is enough to make the critic reach for his gun. To exterminate this particular breed of fungus from the English theatre is not merely a duty; it is a pleasure.

In the course of this essay I have referred to *the play of ideas*. By this I mean a play which has something to sell, which has some quite simple point to make, and I should advocate the writing of such plays, not as the only means of renewing the inspiration of our theatre, but as the easiest piece of advice that can be given to budding playwrights. Everybody cannot be a poet or even a particularly powerful writer, but everybody can *think* and can give to their play a hard rational core which will eliminate the purely decorative element and make for a strong simplicity of theme. Obviously the success of any such endeavour will be in proportion to the talents of the writer, but thought in a play will at least serve as an antidote to many of the principal evils of the contemporary theatre.

And it is only fair to face the full consequences of this advocacy of the play of ideas. It might equally well be called the *play of propaganda*, and I should be prepared to welcome the name, if only to start an argument. Propaganda; yes, in the same way as Shaw's *Applecart* or Brecht's *Mother Courage* are propaganda. Both Shaw and Brecht use the stage as a medium for advocating their ideas about life and, more especially, the society in which they lived. But did anyone ever suppose that the theatre should be divorced from contemporary society and its problems? These are, in fact, the very things with which the theatre should deal, the very fields in which it has won some of its greatest triumphs. At the minute there are no fundamental political problems in this country, so it is difficult to put politics on the stage, but there are social problems and they should certainly be used as dramatic material.

Moreover it should not be assumed that, in putting on plays that deal with contemporary problems or have a strong content of contemporary thought, the dramatist is necessarily condemning himself to a kind of naturalist hell. Brecht has shown that what he calls 'narrative realism' can get away from the three-walled room of the average nineteenth century naturalist set without losing anything in urgency or force. What is being advocated here is not naturalism but realism, a connexion between the theatre and life produced, in this instance, by the expression of a coherent body of ideas (given the fact that the only ideas a dramatist can possibly express are those which are, in some sense, 'living' in his own epoch). Of course, as I have already said, we have to watch quality very carefully; Mr Morgan's play *The Burning Glass* dealt with a question that is indeed central to the thought of our time (what is to be done with discoveries like the hydrogen bomb?), but it dealt with it in a way that was so false that, just because of the importance of the theme, it was bound to be criticized harshly by the

very people who might otherwise have welcomed it as a
worthy attempt. One pre-condition of choosing a theme
that can be called realist is that you must be realist to the
end. Otherwise there is only disaster to follow.

Of course the play of ideas or the play of propaganda or
the social play (for all these are related to one another) are
not the only way to achieve a heightened contact with real
life. There is also poetry. My objection to Mr Fry is simply
that I do not consider him a good enough poet to write
verse drama, but I have no objection to the poetic play as
such. It is indeed the highest form to be seen on the stage,
but it is not much use for the critic to advocate it as a cure
for present discontents, since it requires genuine poets, and
these can only be prayed for, not created. The English
poetic theatre is slowly (and largely due to the efforts of
T. S. Eliot) fighting its way out of a situation of great
difficulty which it inherited from the Victorians. The divorce
between poetic language and ordinary speech which is felt
with peculiar force in Tennyson's or Browning's plays, as
well as the traditional reverence for Shakespeare, had by
the end of the nineteenth century produced an attitude of
mind on the part of the public towards poetic drama which
regarded it as necessarily archaic and necessarily avoiding
anything too nearly approaching contemporary life. It was
reduced to the status of a costume drama conducted in
iambic pentameters, and the distrust of it ever since has been
such that only three ways have so far been found of reintro-
ducing the poetic element to the English stage. The first
is having poetic words spoken by primitives who might
normally be expected to speak like that (or so the public
can be induced to imagine); Synge's *Riders to the Sea* is a
case in point. The second is by the creation of a theatre of
ritual. Mr Eliot's *Murder in the Cathedral*, for instance,
would not shock an audience in the same way as poetry
on an ordinary stage since most people are used to hearing
a kind of poetry recited in church. Lastly, the same writer's
Cocktail Party and *Confidential Clerk* represent an attempt to,

as it were, smuggle in poetry without his audience being aware of what is happening to them. They sit down to a West End cocktail comedy and, lo and behold! before they know where they are they are imbibing poetry. Such, at least, is the theory, and, whatever its defects in practice may be, anyone concerned with the theatre can only be grateful to Mr Eliot for abandoning the (for him) safe ground of ritualistic drama and embarking on the more dangerous task of enlarging the range of the poetic play.

However, Mr Eliot has also spoken of a point at which the poetic dramatist 'can dare to make more liberal use of poetry and take greater liberties with ordinary colloquial speech', and, if poetry is to return to the stage, audiences must be able to swallow it straight. Here the way ahead lies via the plays of Lorca and perhaps some of those of Yeats and Claudel. The mixture of verse and prose in a play like *Blood Wedding* should mislead nobody; it is poetry through-out. This tale of how, on the burning sierras, one man carries off another's bride on his horse and of how they then fight to the death, so that only the women of the family are left at the end to weep for them, is told entirely by the poetry. The opposition of two worlds, of the fertile world of women and the sterile world of death where men fight with small, glittering knives beneath a cold moon is only the more poignant since the one leads inevitably to the other. It is the horse, supreme symbol of passion and procreation and also the death symbol, in whose image the two worlds are connected and in some sort reconciled. Men would not be men, there would be no creation, if they did not love and fight for the love and die for it. The horse is at once the risk, the reward and the penalty—everything that comes from the acceptance of the condition of arrogant, passionate humanity—and the wealth and beauty of this symbolism are such that they leave one reeling in the amazement that only comes before a great work of art. A play where the meaning is entirely carried by the poetry—that is the way our poetic drama should go. Or are we so lost that birth and love and death can no longer strike chords in the English language?

Perhaps Spanish is a more primitive, less worn language than English, but great poetic plays have been written in France and England during the twentieth century. *Partage de Midi* and perhaps the second *Tête d'Or* seem to me to establish Claudel's title to fame as a poetic dramatist, and though these plays were in fact written some fifty years ago *Le Soulier de Satin*, that huge cosmos *manqué*, is more recent. In Yeats's *Purgatory* and *Death of Cuchulain* there are also visible the seeds of a type of poetic drama which has yet to be developed. These examples give some grounds for hope that poetry may one day return to the stage in force, but that day will not come unless critics are prepared to scrutinize narrowly the quality of the verse presented to them. The great poetic dramatist is the great poet. This cannot be too often repeated.

There is a third type of play which has recently been elaborated in France and of which we may see something in this country, though English writers tend to be hostile to anything too overtly philosophical. This is what might be called *the play of metaphysical situation*. Its characteristics are, first, an attempt to express the entire human situation and a refusal to regard anything outside that basic situation as having any importance. Secondly, it follows from this that the nature of the drama will be essentially static and that the only departures from this will take place in the violence which ensues when the ordinary conventions of the world of appearances are fractured. Thirdly, since the most usual of these conventions is language, the writers of this type of play have generally attempted a sort of dissolution of speech, whether by dissolving it into pure nonsense or else by reducing it to the lowest level of banality (the deliberate imbecility of the dialogue in Arthur Adamov's *Le Ping-Pong* is a case in point). This kind of play (we have already seen Eugene Ionesco's *La Leçon* and Samuel Beckett's *En Attendant Godot* in London) presents considerable interest, since it is an attempt to express in terms of the stage philosophical intuitions which might seem at first sight to be quite undramatic. However, for this very reason, it can probably only flourish where there is already a strong interest in *avant-garde* theatre. It is probably not suited to be a remedy for a sickly stage.

*   *   *

I have indicated some of the directions in which I believe the future of the serious play to lie, but the problem of attracting young writers to experiment along these lines still remains. As I have hinted above, a solution depends to a large extent on producers. There are a number of people in London doing good work for the theatre (the Arts Theatre and Theatre Workshop, for instance, both put on interesting plays), but I doubt if anyone has yet given much thought to the question of creating playwrights. A great producer today would take as much trouble with his writers as with his actors, and this would involve going out to look for them in the first place. It would also mean getting hold of promising writers and persuading them to have a go at a play. It would not be an easy thing to do, and would probably require more intellectual calibre than many people at present associated with the theatre possess, but I feel fairly certain it would pay off. Then, when he had found his plays, the producer could assemble a company and put them on—in a garret if necessary. In the past it has always been a concerted effort on the part of people with no money, but with time and talent and ideas to give, that has created a theatre. It could be so again, but one of the most important partners in this co-operative concern must not be left outside in the cold. The writer must be brought into the theatre, since it is his absence that is so sorely felt at the moment.

*   *   *

In this essay I have tried to state a problem without being too dogmatic about possible solutions. Indeed, I am not very sure that there is any solution. What I am certain of is that critics, who blame the present state of the English theatre on its (admittedly bad) economic organization, are starting at the wrong end. The threatened decline of the English theatre from art to entertainment will not be remedied by tax relief or a break-up of the big theatre chains. The inability of the theatre to attract new talent to serve it is due to far more fundamental causes and has been accompanied by a serious drop in standards. For every time a worthless play is excused on the grounds of being 'good theatre' a real betrayal is taking place. All art exists on a common level of serious concern with life. Once that is eliminated, all that is left is a painted husk—no art at all. At the present moment there is nothing going on in the English theatre which will be of the slightest interest to anyone ten—let alone fifty—years later. The last original impulse it received dates from before 1914, and to talk of good theatre when what you mean is the exhausted repetition of techniques which have been practised over a decline of forty years is to blind oneself to reality. Blindness is characteristic of the decadence of an art, but, for that very reason, lack of self-criticism should not be allowed to continue. The English theatre has got away with far too much for far too long. We must try to put matters right.

Atmosphere

*

by Philip Hope-Wallace

THERE IS NO logic about it. You may go to the
theatre for 'entertainment', just as a mountaineer
might be said to risk his life on the Matterhorn for 'exercise'.
We analyse the passions at best weakly. I dare say many
people are wise in preferring not to analyse them at all.
Ware wheezing Proust and his too withering gaze into what
makes our hearts well up (or sink again). But with so much
drama that is not theatre and so much of it so near to hand
—the TV screen, the cinema, the radio play—and with so
many Jeremiahs prophesying the imminent doom of the
theatre proper, or improper (as most prophets have it),
it becomes perhaps a duty to try to understand in what
consists a 'love of theatre' which in less urgent times might
be left unexplained and happy.

We are taught to look back to childhood by analysts of
all schools. Can this twitch upon the thread I feel, this
magnetic attraction to the whole field of the theatre (so that
I orient my feet even in a foreign town almost by instinct
to the theatre—and that sometimes at the most untheatrical
hours, mid-morning, longing to see at least posters and steps
leading to the arcane temple), can it be that these are the
dividends of repression?

Not at the least in my own case history. My first Barrie,
Peter Pan with a Peter I could no doubt date precisely, was
a reality lived in the acme of *suspended belief* (those flying
wires!) and it was an early experience. My parents never
thought it wrong for me to see or read a 'good' play and
my piping voice would often hush the nursery table with

requests for explanations of some of the cross talk in such plays as *Measure for Measure*. It was on the contrary the cinema which was forbidden. I knew a surreptitious furtive longing for those dark and flickering abodes, scented with sandalwood and loud with tinkling pianism. But to be locked out from a cinema today I could support with an equanimity only measurable to being told that the TV had broken down just before the big fight. To be locked out of a theatre, to be told categorically that there is not even one tiny standing place available, is to know the torment of love spurned.

Love clearly enters into it. The point I wish to make is that I am also partial to a good film. But in the last analysis it must be love. On the doing-without principle, I would suffer no sorrow to be excluded from Lords as no doubt many a white-gloved debutante would happily find that she had mislaid the tickets for *Tristan und Isolde*, for me a fatality unthinkable. So let us agree that love does enter into the calculation.

And young conditioning. There, I fear, we are up against a more serious problem. Having invoked Proust, if only as a warning, I turned back just now to the pages he conse-crates to his first visit to see *La Berma* (Bernhardt). No analysis, rather plain reporting. And vivid enough to any-one who recalls similar treats which somehow a little cheated expectation. There was the social agony of it: the idea that the audience by ill manners or apathy would cause the star to dim her light or the other players to give a poor performance. Then, indignation that more was not being felt by the audience. And above all that little secret mistake we have all made at one time or another in the theatre: mistaking some secondary player for the star, lavishing on this first-seen our pent-up admiration and then knowing humiliation when, anon, there enters the greater luminary, greeted by storms of applause which put us (the duped) slightly agin' her. That moment remembered by the young Marcel is the moment dramatic criticism as a craft may find its roots. But the famous page does not explain the passion for the living theatre itself and I rather doubt if Proust himself felt it.

For, does a passion for the theatre grow in later life (as well some passions do)? Or is it acquired young or not at all? Lecturing to groups of young persons whose experience is almost solely of the cinema, I have found that what seems to discourage their further experiments in theatre-going is nearly always that they cannot really either see or hear. The close-up, the amplified sound-track have blunted appetites none too keen before. The idea that players may have to project their voices or their expressions comes surprisingly to those who accept as a right thirty-two-foot views of Miss Joan Crawford and 'the miracle of Stereophonic Sound'.

I have to remember this when in the theatre I hear (as increasingly I do hear) people talking to one another during the course of a play in perfectly normal, clear conversational voices. I cannot imagine myself ever speaking above a sub-stage whisper, once the curtain was up on that warmest of all hearths, a living stage. But such talkers feel no impiety. It is simply that they do not feel that they are any part of the ritual make-belief 'up there'. They cannot imagine that the ritual might cease or slow up or fail altogether as the result of inattention or indifference on their part. And there, I believe, you have the quintessence: for a play does not become a play until it is being lived *by permission of the audience*.

Now I beg to be acquitted of mysticism in this matter, and do not want to drool of two-way electric currents passing from player to audience and back; nor to dwell on Audience Participation, which often means no more than cheerleaders' laugh-cues, the clacque or, worse still, those actors-in-our-midst productions in open-stage theatres where Œdipus comes groping past you in your stall or Falstaff clouts you on the neck. But a mutual awareness, the actor's sense of playing upon an audience and of an audience pulling for the emotion which they expect of him, for the surprises indeed which they half expect of him —of such is the realm of the living drama. No shadows on a wall, not even live players, coiled like Laocoon in television cables athwart a cathode tube, are ever going to create the same effect. And immediately we have to add: nor risk such total failure.

Perhaps that then is simply it. When this chance miracle works, the knowing that we the audience are surrendering to an illusion which hangs upon a thread which may at any second snap, it is the sheer risk of the whole thing that delights. Yes, and the power. For in our audience's hands, as well as theirs (the actors'), lies this profane miracle of the true theatrical illusion.

And here one cannot avoid pointing out that it is a shared pleasure, a communion. The language of revivalism comes easily on critics and must be filtered cautiously. But the theatre in origin was religious and still is so, even those orphic rites at the Palladium when Danny Kaye or Johnnie Ray 'appear'. True, few people have not known times when they would have given much to behave like poor queer Ludwig II and have the play presented to them alone in a private theatre. Those who have sat through school matinee *Macbeth*'s or endured the contemptuous coughing of a London first night smarties' audience reacting unfavourably to Chekov must have cursed their fellows in the audience. But this is an aberration. The theatre is a place of common spells and collective emotions. Ideally all 'houses' should be hushed and yet pulsing with excitement. The single watcher, the mono-audience belongs to the world of radio communication, the world of the written word too perhaps. I would make it plain that my feelings on entering a theatre are other than those on entering a library or switching on a 'set'.

No doubt my feelings are what William James would class as numinous. This does not mean that I feel for any auditorium what no doubt a devotee feels even for the blue marvels of Chartres, the gigantic 'set' of St Peter's, Rome, or a corrugated iron conventicle. I do not quickly summon the genius loci. To stand in the Colosseum even, or amid the thyme and bees in the great theatre at Leptis Magna or bump my head happily among the 'perspectives' of the Teatro Olimpico at Vicenza have not, I confess, always sprung my imagination as I could have wished. To think 'Here in this very place how many humans must have sat to laugh and weep' is a thought which has come hard. But some such feeling does indeed often descend in the most unexpected theatres, or even at the contemplation of some fetish object, a fan, a tattered programme or ballet shoe. Earlier generations called it 'The smell of grease-paint'. Today the word 'Atmosphere' unsatisfactorily must serve—and having pressed it into service, I must look round half sadly, as when the house lights go up again, and admit that it is 'Atmosphere' precisely which I cannot, and have not here, defined.

The Gardener's Lament

The Entr'acte of Giraudoux's *Electra*

Until recently the plays of Jean Giraudoux (1882–1944) have never had the successes they deserved with English-speaking audiences, and only Amphitryon 38, *thanks to the performances of the Lunts, had any real success before the war. In the last few years, however, Giraudoux, the most polished stylist and perhaps most French of all modern French writers, has been translated and played with marked success on both sides of the Atlantic. His play* Ondine *proved a big draw on Broadway, and* The Enchanted *and Christopher Fry's adaptation of* La Guerre de Troie n'aura pas Lieu *have introduced him to the British public.*

Giraudoux's universe, unlike more recent French writers', is a universe where optimism abounds, where man has faith in life in spite of all its imperfections, where darkness, like life, is transitory. His drama is always conceived on two planes, the real and the illusory, the world as it is and the world that might be. There is no dividing line, no iron curtain between the one and the other. Just as life leads to death, so, as the gardener in his play *Electra beautifully expresses it, 'the trouble is, I always say what is slightly the opposite of what I want to say'.*

Giraudoux's plays are anti-naturalistic and have that breadth of imagination and sweep of creative power which is so lacking in the naturalist theatre today. Here, in Lothian Small's translation, is 'The Gardener's Lament', the entr'acte of *Electra. The gardener addresses himself to the audience confidentially, and outlines not only what the play is about, but Giraudoux's own belief in living.*

THE GARDENER: I am no longer in it. That is why I am free to come and tell you what the play never could. In stories of this kind they won't stop killing and biting one another just to let you know that life has only one objective, love. To see the parricide, with his dagger already poised, stopping to sing to you the praises of love would not be right. It would seem artificial. Many would not believe it. But I, standing here amid all this abandon, this desolation, I do not really see what else there is to do.

21

And I am speaking quite impartially. I shall never be reconciled to marrying anyone but Electra, and I shall never have Electra. I am made for living day and night with a woman, and I shall always live by myself. So as to give myself unremittingly at any time or season and always I shall keep myself prepared. It is my wedding night that I am spending here, quite alone—thank you for being here—and I shall never have another, and the orange juice I had prepared for Electra, it is I who ought to have drunk it;—there is not a drop left, it was a long wedding night. So who would doubt my word! The trouble is, I always say what is slightly the opposite of what I want to say, but it would really be hopeless today, with my heart so sad and such bitterness in my mouth— come to think of it, oranges are bitter—if I were for one moment to forget that I have to speak to you about joy. Yes, joy and love. They are preferable, I come to tell you, to bitterness and hate. A kind of motto to work out on a porch or on a scarf or a clump of dwarf begonias. Obviously life is a blunder, but it is very fine, is life. Obviously nothing ever works, nothing is ever settled; but you must admit that now and then things work admirably, are settled admirably. . . . Not for me. . . . Or rather for me. . . . Judging by the desire to love, the ability to love everything and everybody, which comes to me from life's greatest misfortune, what must it be for those who have lesser misfortunes! What love must be felt by those men who marry wives they do not love, what joy by those who, after spending an hour at home, are deserted by the women they adore, what admiration by parents whose children are too ugly. Obviously it was not very gay tonight, my garden, but it can be remembered as a little festivity. It was not much good my pretending at times that Electra was beside me, speaking to her, saying: Come in, Electra! Are you cold, Electra? It took nobody in, not even the dog, far less myself. He promised us a bride, thought the dog, and he trots out a word. My master has

married a word; he went and put on his white suit—the
one I can't play with him in because it shows the marks
of my paws—only to marry a word. He scolds me when
I bark at shadows, I mean real shadows, for they don't
exist, and there he goes and tries to kiss a word. So I
didn't lie down. Me lie down with a word!—that was too
much for me. With a word you can speak, and that's all.
But squatting as I do in the garden, with everything going
a little astray at night, the moon in tow with the sundial,
and the blind owl drinking at the gravel path instead of
the stream, you would have understood what I understood, namely, the truth. You would have understood on
the day your parents died, that your parents were born;
on the day you were ruined, that you were rich; on the day
your child was ungrateful, that he was gratitude itself; on
the day you were deserted, that the whole world was
coming at you in a rush of tenderness. That is just what
was happening to me in this empty silent suburb. They
came hurtling themselves on me, all those petrified trees,
those unmoving hills.

And all that applies to this play. You certainly cannot
say that Electra is the ideal object for Clytemnestra's love.
But even so a distinction must be drawn. Electra is
looking for a mother. She would make a mother of the
first comer. She married me because she felt that I was
the only man, absolutely the only one, who could be a
sort of mother. And for that matter I am not the only
one. There are men who would be delighted to be in
child nine months to have girls—every man. Nine months
is a bit long, but to be in child a week, say, a day, there's
not a man but would be proud of it. It may be that in
thus looking for her mother inside her mother she would
have to open her bosom to her, but among kings that is
rather theoretical. With kings lots of experiments come
off which never come off among the common people,
pure hatred, pure anger. It always is purity. That is what
tragedy really is, with its incest, its parricide: purity,

that is, in a word, innocence. I don't know if you are like me. But to me, in tragedy, the pharaoh who commits suicide says hope, the marshal who turns traitor says faith, the duke who commits murder says charity. It is an exercise of love, cruelty . . . I mean Tragedy. That is why I am sure this morning that if I were only to ask it, the heavens would give me their approval, would give a sign, that there is a miracle quite ready which would show you inscribed on the sky and have you repeat my motto of the lonely forsaken man: joy and love. If you like I'll ask it. I'm as sure as I am here now that a voice from on high would answer me, that sound-boxes and amplifiers and the thunders of God—God, if I want them, holds them all in readiness to shout aloud at my command: joy and love. But take my advice, better not ask me to. To begin with, it would be more seemly. It is not for a gardener to be asking God for a storm, even of compassion. And then it is not much use. One feels so strongly that at this moment, and yesterday, and tomorrow, and all the time, they are all up there, and even if they are only one, and even if that one happened to be absent, they are all ready to shout joy and love. It is so much more dignified in a man to take the Gods at their word—at their word is a euphemism—not to make them dot the i's and cross the t's, to become involved and establish between the parties the relations of creditor and debtor. With me it has always been the silence I found reassuring. . . . Yes I'll ask them not to shout joy and love, don't you think? If they absolutely want to, then let them. But I entreat them rather, I entreat you, God, in proof of your affection, to use your voice and shouting to make a silence, one second of your silence. It is so much more convincing. Listen. . . . Thank you.

Music as Drama's Handmaid

*

by Eric Blom

MUSIC is a more than great enough art to be self-sufficient, and in some of its manifestations — chamber or symphonic music, for instance—it can be arrogantly so. Those who do not cherish it for its own sake then find that they have no use for it. Yet it does not cold-shoulder them for that. It can quite humbly serve in a subordinate capacity: by heightening the enjoyment of food, by giving rhythmic substance to a dance, by enlivening festivity of one sort or another, by giving greater depth to worship. In performing some of these functions it may reduce quality to such unpretentiousness as to make it quite negligible in itself, and yet it may still be of value.

An important service to be rendered by music that specially concerns us here is that of enhancing the performance of a play. In a sense any theatrical production seems left in the cold without musical assistance of some kind, even if it only takes the form of some light pieces played before the opening and during intervals by a handful of instruments, called an orchestra by a quite quixotic extension of courtesy, or perhaps just a piano or two. But this is a mere expedient, not to be taken seriously, and we need not be unduly indignant if, instead of being listened to in solemn silence by an audience, such entertainment is regarded as no more than a stimulant for conversation. The more the music insists on being heard, the louder grows that chatter, quite automatically; and though earnest persons periodically protest and declare this to be an indication of the frivolity, barbarism and stupidity of theatregoers, they may be reminded that people go to a play to enjoy acting and, perhaps, to interest themselves in a dramatist's ideas or take pleasure in some form of beauty proper to the stage, but are entitled to relax between the acts and must not be expected to turn temporarily into concert audiences.

Difficulties begin, however, when for once a musician of distinction, if not of eminence, has been commissioned to write incidental music for some play or other that seems to the producer to call for a composer's aid in much the same way as it calls for a stage designer's. It is not easy even now to forget the furious indignation that seized upon Delius in 1923, when Basil Dean produced Flecker's *Hassan* with his exquisitely poetical if not dramatically very apt music, and it was found on most evenings to be hopelessly drowned in conversation—if the usual cackle resounding from stalls to gallery can be fairly called that. It is galling indeed to think of such fine taste and arduous work so largely wasted on unresponsive ears, though even here one must make allowances for those members of not specifically musical audiences who could hardly be expected to realize that here, suddenly, was interval music to be taken seriously. The tradition of its usual unimportance was too strong.

A serious tradition of theatre music has never taken firm root in England, in spite of several good beginnings, and when for once in a way a composer like Sullivan or Edward German was engaged to provide it for Shakespearian and occasionally other productions, he himself found that tradition so weak that he contented himself deliberately with work showing neat craftsmanship but no sort of profundity. Indeed, even relevance to the play in hand was hardly considered, and when it was attempted, as in German's 'Henry VIII' and 'Nell Gwyn' dances, the result was sham antiques such as are now fit only to decorate the palm-courts and restaurants of hotels ambitious enough to provide musical entertainment with tea and dinner. Norman O'Neill, during his long years as musical director of the

Haymarket Theatre, did write music for a great number
and variety of plays which, besides being extremely well
turned out, was apt in style and atmosphere; but he knew
his theatre audience too well to have any illusion that more
than a handful of people each night paid more than the most
superficial attention to his work or was so much as aware
that it was written purposely to suit special requirements.
Still, as most of the plays at the Haymarket had long runs,
the handfuls mounted up to enough to have made O'Neill's
careful work worth while, even though he knew that in the
nature of things it was ephemeral. More serious efforts
made by Stanford and Parry to fit music to Greek plays did
not concern the public theatre but the universities, where
Aeschylus, Sophocles, Euripides and Aristophanes were
acted in the original by undergraduates. Their scores were
even more evanescent than O'Neill's; on the other
hand, from Vaughan Williams's music for *The Wasps* of
Aristophanes a delightful overture has been saved for the
concert-room. Such salvage does occasionally occur in
the history of theatre music, and makes it the more worth
while for a composer to undertake.

A phase more profitable to music in the history of English
drama was its heyday in Elizabethan times. A great deal
was made then of music integrated into plays rather than,
strictly speaking, incidental: the many songs they contained
as a feature of their style were of course sung, and there
was a good deal of stage music that took, so to speak, part
in the action—sennets and tuckets for ceremonial entries,
processional and battle pieces, ghostly music played by
various instruments off-stage or under the stage, and the
like. But there was no entertainment music extraneous to
the play with which the production was in any way concerned. This was on the other hand a great feature of the
Restoration stage, for which Purcell and others wrote their
act-tunes: pieces in dance or song forms in the modish style
of the day, quite independent of the play's character, period
or setting, which were presumably listened to since some

very ingenious craftsmanship was often expended on them. It cannot be said, though, that these pieces were given during the intervals, exactly; they were heard immediately before the rise of the curtain on each act.

Spain and France both had theatre music early, for Calderón and Lope de Vega, for Racine and Molière, and so on. The Spanish classical theatre treated music in much the same way as the English Elizabethan school did. The choruses in Racine's *Esther* and *Athalie*, for instance, were set to music and sung, and some of the more artificial Molière comedies almost became musical plays, though the dialogue vastly predominated.

That Germany in the nineteenth century developed a strong tradition of incidental music on a large scale, fully orchestrated, was not so much due to a wider cultivation of music in general among Germans and Austrians at the time as to peculiar social and theatrical conditions. Many small courts had firmly established private theatres at which, for economy's sake, opera and drama alternated, and they were imitated by numerous cities and towns of various sizes, who thus maintained municipal theatres on the same lines. This meant that, since a large orchestra had to be part of the establishment for the performance of opera, it was on the spot all the time and might as well be kept as busy as possible for its pay. Thus when a play, especially a classic, was to be given, a composer could be encouraged to write incidental music on a lavish scale and to score it for as big an orchestra as the theatre possessed. Beethoven's music for Goethe's *Egmont* at the Vienna Burgtheater (1810) is a classic instance, and Mendelssohn, during his appointment to the Prussian court in Berlin (1841-45), was commissioned to write music for two tragedies by Sophocles, for Shakespeare's *Midsummer Night's Dream* (adding many numbers to the overture of his adolescence which was not written for a theatre) and for Racine's *Athalie*.

In the twentieth century the German-speaking countries fell somewhat behind in the matter of stage music, and for a time, mainly about the 1920's and 1930's, the lead was taken by Paris. But other European nations also showed a growing interest in music as part of theatre-craft, and so do nowadays the United States, where modern American plays especially are provided with it by the younger and more advanced composers.

* * *

The history of theatre music is a large subject. What has been shown here is no more than a few landmarks; and what must now be attempted is a brief outline of what can and should be done by composers who undertake to serve the stage. The first thing they must certainly grasp is that they have to be content to serve and must on no account try to domineer. They need not submit too abjectly to a producer who wishes to dictate to them, and indeed there is little danger of that, since no man of the theatre is likely to know enough about music to be able to give detailed directions, though he may know what he wants or at any rate think he does. But there must be more give than take. The whole production will have to be timed, and that can be done only, in broad outlines at any rate, by the stage director. However urgent the pressure of inspiration, the composer will not be able to let himself go on a long symphonic interlude between two acts or scenes if it does not seem desirable to prolong the performance beyond the extent of the text, and if there is a question of filling up a minute or two during a change of scene it may be necessary to halt the creative impulse with a stop-watch, however irksome that may be to genius in labour, or else to make a cut in a piece already written down that is found to have overshot the allowable time. Then there may be incidents in the play for which the composer is itching to write down music already kindled in him by a spark of an idea, but where the producer wants to get on with the action without interference from what he regards as only one of the attendant arts called in to help where he needs help, and which indeed for the purpose in hand *is* a satellite art, however much the musician may revolt against such a notion. On the other hand the producer may wish to suspend action at a given moment and ask for music to give significance to the pause or to bridge a technically unavoidable time-lapse, where the composer feels that he has nothing to give spontaneously. If so, he must be prepared to do what he can by deliberation and calculation, to let professional skill take control where inspiration will not be commanded. It can be done, and very often, if it is done with determination and without any stiff-necked disdain of a menial task, inspiration of some sort will suddenly make its appearance unbidden. If not, skill alone will serve, provided the composer has enough of it.

Not every kind of play calls for music with equal urgency, and some kinds cannot conceivably do with it. If we remember Ibsen's *Peer Gynt*, for instance, and Grieg's music for it, we can hardly help feeling that two artists were born and made for each other, in spite of the fact that the Grieg music, with all its suitability, quite fails to measure up to the greatness of the play—and here, perhaps, is an indication to the musician that a certain humility is a virtue in those who undertake to associate with the drama. But *Peer Gynt* is poetic drama and needs music to heighten its poetry. If on the other hand we think of Ibsen's sociological problem plays, we find it difficult if not impossible to imagine what kind of music could possibly serve them; and the embarrassing paradox is that any performance of them, which is bound to be a serious matter, is for that very reason doomed to become associated with irrelevant interval music of the most unsuitable kind imaginable. The alternative is cold silence, which in its way is just as bad. To the question of how music is to serve realistic drama there is no satisfactory answer, for the simple reason that it can have no proper function there. Light domestic comedies, detective plays, farces, and so on, have no room for integrated music either, but certainly need the lowliest sort of service music can render during intervals. There is no problem here, however: anything will do, provided it has no particular importance in itself and does not claim attention for its own sake.

Of all the world's great plays, however, a surprisingly small number are purely realistic, and any that are not will be the more impressive for having music specially provided for them, while not a few can be said to be hardly capable of existing without it. Greek tragedy, the Spanish picaresque theatre, the English Elizabethans and Jacobeans, the French seventeenth-century classics, Goethe's *Faust* and all the nineteenth-century romanticism it leads to, down to Kaiser and the rest of the expressionists, the psychologized ancient legendary of Giraudoux and Obey, the delicate prose fantasies of Anouilh, the new English verse drama of Eliot, Duncan and Fry, the American experiments of O'Neill, Saroyan and others—all this cries out for some kind of assistance from music, and music above all willing to assume the temporary function of handmaid to a sister-art. Loudest of all are still the cries of Shakespeare. The productions at the Old Vic in London, for instance, have shown how indispensable it is to provide each one with a complement of music, more or less extended, more or less fitting, or more or less distinguished, as requirements and luck may decree. It has become a regular habit there to commission a new score for every revival, and composers are wise who, instead of complaining of subordination, recognize here a new outlet for their gifts which, while it can be irksome in details, also opens up all manner of fascinating possibilities.

The French Dramatic Centres

*

by Michel Saint-Denis

The Dramatic Centres in France are an exciting new development. Between 1947 and 1952 five have been established in the different regions : the Eastern Dramatic Centre with its headquarters at Strasbourg, the Comédie of St Etienne, the Western Dramatic Centre (at Rennes), the Comédie of Provence (at Aix-en-Provence) and the Grenier of Toulouse. They are geographically situated so as to serve nearly the whole of France. M. Saint-Denis, who is director of the Eastern Dramatic Centre, surveys here the aims and purposes of the Dramatic Centre movement, which has so successfully challenged the tendency of theatres to close down by proving that there is a public for good theatre—everywhere. Here is a movement run by enthusiasts with the faith of a mission— to bring all that is best in the living traditions of the theatre to everybody, wherever they may be.

BEFORE explaining the circumstances which brought about the creation of the French Dramatic Centres, it is perhaps best to try and define what we mean by a Dramatic Centre. We give this name to a company of players, supported by the State and the local municipality, whose purpose is to bring a worth-while theatre, with a classical repertoire of French and foreign plays, to the towns in its neighbouring region, and with the long-term aim of stimulating there original theatrical activity. We shall examine this definition later on, but at the outset it will be seen that the Dramatic Centres satisfy a specifically French need, and if we are to explain this need we must take a rapid glance at past history.

France before the Revolution of 1789 was composed of provinces each having its own autonomy, political, administrative, financial and, as a consequence, cultural. Thus if we take Lyons, a city of printers and publishers, for example, or Dijon, the capital of the Dukes of Burgundy, Avignon, the Papal residence, Aix-en-Provence, the seat of the Counts of Provence—in those days such cities were veritable miniature capitals each having its own artistic tradition. From the sixteenth century onwards, the policy of Francis I laid the foundations of absolute monarchy by depriving the chief aristocratic families in the country of their power. This was the beginning of the decline of the French provinces and the rise of Paris, which was to become not only the political capital of France, but her intellectual and artistic centre as well. This centralization, peculiar to France, was further enforced by the 'Versailles' statecraft of Louis XIV, then by the Revolution and the Empire, which divided up the old provinces and substituted for them the *départements*, administrative units under the authority of prefects controlled directly by Paris.

Little by little the patronage of the kings drew the best artists from the rest of France to Paris, where they settled. Paris gave and still gives them glory, fame and money; it is in Paris that you find the best museums, the best libraries, the best concerts and the best theatres; Paris is where the youth congregates, which produces that clash of ideas which makes intellectual life possible. But this centralization has progressively sterilized the provinces. As soon as a young man shows any talent he leaves his native town, where there are no openings, to try his luck in Paris. In this way the vicious circle has been drawn, for the provinces have become suspicious of their own coin and only welcome what has already won the approval of the Paris critics, who make and despatch reputations. The result of this state of affairs is that it is impossible for an artist to carry on a career in the provinces. The few great provincial artists, such as Mistral, that France has had in the last century have been sanctioned by Paris.

The intellectual and artistic radiation of Paris is not in

c

question, but I feel it wise to stress that this galaxy of so many talents and potentialities which attracts so many artists and foreign art lovers to Paris is detrimental to the artistic life of the rest of the country.

*   *   *

This situation was particularly serious for the theatre. In addition to subsidized theatres there are forty-eight legitimate theatres in Paris, and before the Centres were started in 1947 these contained practically the whole of the theatrical life of the country. Such intense theatrical activity may be cause for satisfaction, but it should be observed that the Paris theatres before the last war were only in touch with a section of the middle classes; they were, in fact, theatres belonging to a class and not to society in general. Most of the playwrights and producers worked to please certain powerful critics on whose verdict the commercial success of the play depended. Confronted by this Parisian efflorescence, the provinces were deprived completely of their theatrical life: the municipal theatres, except for some opera houses which always had the same nineteenth-century operas on their boards, no longer employed any regular dramatic companies. Theatre after theatre closed its doors, and there were only the touring companies which brought Paris successes. And even the Paris circuits only visited the most important cities; the other towns, without a theatre (hardly any theatres were built in the provinces between 1900 and 1939), were completely deprived of live performances. The people of Alsace, Brittany or Provence no longer had the means of portraying on the stage their own way of life, and only amateurs—among them some promising ones— gave continuity to the theatre, in spite of innumerable difficulties and general indifference.

*   *   *

This survey would not be accurate, however, without mention of those people in the French theatre who before

1914 had tried to challenge this trend and, in spite of failure, had shown a way which was to be explored later on. Among them was Firmin Gémier, who in 1912 founded the Théâtre Ambulant and after the 1914 war the Théâtre National Populaire. The Théâtre Ambulant only lasted two seasons and the T.N.P., lacking sufficient funds and badly supported by a public which had still hardly been discovered, remained half paralysed until Jean Vilar, twenty years later, was able to supply what was missing: a style of production and a new public.

If the tentative efforts of Gémier were rather of a sociological order, the work of Copeau had been above all æsthetic. It attacked first out-of-date stage conventions. It is not my task here to write the history of the Vieux-Colombier, but I would like to quote a few lines from Jacques Copeau which seem to me to sum up the main ideas of a revolution which was going to reform the contemporary theatre: 'Stage conventions must not be mistaken for dramatic conventions. Abolishing the former does not liberate you from the latter, on the contrary. Bowing to the requirements of the stage and its crude physical equipment can be a discipline obliging us to put the whole emphasis on the acts and the feelings of our characters. Let the other illusions fade away, for our new productions give us a bare trestle.'

This bare trestle was the famous permanent set of the Vieux-Colombier. But in 1924 the Vieux-Colombier had to close down, and Jacques Copeau retired with a number of actors and pupils to Burgundy. In this way the Copiaus was born, a school of actors, which was the forerunner of the future Dramatic Centres. Living among the wine growers, the Copiaus performed in the villages of Burgundy classical farces, adaptations of old works and new pieces written by Copeau himself or by members of the group. These new works, accompanied by songs, dances and improvisations, had often taken their themes from the surroundings in which the actors and audience lived—such as the production called *The Working of the Vineyard*. In 1929 the Copiaus disbanded, but the seed had been sown, and twenty years later two former Copiaus were directing the Centres, Jean Dasté and myself.

* * *

Such was the background and such were the cultural traditions which gave rise to the creation of the Centres. They were born to meet a need which was growing more and more urgent, animated by the zeal of the courageous pioneers, and everything was ready when the public bodies lent their support to their establishment. In the years which followed the Liberation a spirit of reform and revival spread throughout the country. Politics might be said to have become theatre-minded, with the organization of dramatic festivals, the granting of subsidies (under the form of tax relief) for those Paris theatres which sought to establish a worth-while theatre, the creation of the *Concours des Jeunes Compagnies*—help for the first play, and so on. These were the first results of a programme which was quite naturally to include the setting up of the Centres.

The first Centre was the *Centre Dramatique de l'Est*, which I now have the privilege of directing. It was established in five towns in the East of France, Colmar, Haguenau, Metz, Mulhouse and Strasbourg, combined in a 'Syndicat Inter-communal'. Talks started with the *Direction des Arts et Lettres* in 1946, and the first performance was given in the municipal theatre of Colmar in January 1947. This was soon followed by the establishment of the *Comédie de St Etienne* in September 1947 (which absorbed the *Comédiens de Grenoble*, founded in 1942); that of the *Grenier de Toulouse* in January 1949 (which had already been in existence as an amateur company since 1945), the *Comédie de l'Ouest* in 1949 and, finally, that of the *Comédie de Provence* in 1952.

All these Centres are situated in towns which possess a university, so that students can form a taste for a theatrical repertoire. All of them are situated in different parts of

France at a considerable distance from Paris and all are
subsidized by the State and the municipality of the city in
which they are established (or the towns which support
them). The subsidies vary according to the Centres: they
have been in 1953, from 29,250,000 francs (£29,250) for the
Centre Dramatique de l'Est to 11,000,000 francs (£11,000)
for that of St Étienne. (In comparison, the subsidy of the
Comédie Française in the same year was 343,000,000 francs.)
In the subsidy, the contribution of the municipalities is of
variable proportion. Thus for the *Centre Dramatique de
l'Est*, each town in the Syndicat Intercommunal pays three
francs a year per inhabitant. In addition, certain towns
where the Centres play support them by taking over the
expenses of the theatre, electricity, stage hands, etc.

The Director of each Centre is proposed by the State,
but his appointment is submitted to the interested municipalities for their consent. He is free to engage the players
and technicians he wishes, free to put on the shows he
chooses; he is responsible to the *Direction des Arts et Lettres*
for the financial conduct of his Centre.

*   *   *

In outlining the different Centres I shall try to explain
the special characteristics of each of them.

LA COMÉDIE DE ST ETIENNE is directed by Jean Dasté.
Jean Dasté is without doubt the figure in the theatre world
with the greatest experience of the Centres, and the man who
has given the longest service to the revival of drama in the
provinces. A former pupil of Jacques Copeau, he was a
member of the *Copiaus*, then of the *Compagnie des Quinze*.
Finally in 1942 he established the *Comédiens de Grenoble*,
a first attempt at a Dramatic Centre, which, after local
difficulties, was transplanted in 1947 to St Etienne.

An actor and producer, Jean Dasté is a remarkable
force and has been able to collect around him a team who
work with a homogeneity which one rarely finds in the
theatre. His company, stationed in a mining region, in

many localities reaches a large working-class public. It serves the Lyonnaise region, the valley of the Rhone, Burgundy and the Alps.

LE CENTRE DRAMATIQUE DE L'OUEST is directed by Hubert Gignoux. When he became director he collaborated with a number of local people who had founded, before his arrival, a first-class group of amateurs with a good number of young actors of ability. The Western Dramatic Centre is stationed at Rennes, covers all the west of France, Brittany, Normandy and the valley of the Loire.

LA COMÉDIE DE PROVENCE is directed by Douking. At the beginning it was founded by Gaston Baty, who at the end of his life retired to Aix-en-Provence with some pupils in order to form a school of dramatic art based on the principles which had made his *Théâtre Montparnasse* famous. Unfortunately he died on the day he was to present the first production. Douking succeeded him. Unlike Jean Dasté and Hubert Gignoux, Douking is not an actor-producer, but a producer-designer. The Comédie of Provence serves the Eastern Midi, and the coast from Perpignan to Nice. This region, in spite of its agreeable climate, is one of the most difficult from the theatre point of view, since the Meridional public traditionally prefer operetta and opera to straight plays.

LE GRENIER DE TOULOUSE is directed by Maurice Sarrazin, also an actor-producer. The Grenier of Toulouse, which works throughout the French Midi from the Atlantic at Bordeaux to the Rhone, deserves special attention, for without doubt it is the Centre which has been most successful. To begin with it was a group of amateurs. This group, directed by Maurice Sarrazin, won in 1946 the first prize in the *Concours des Jeunes Compagnies*. Its fame soon passed regional boundaries to give it a national and even an international reputation. Assured of their future by the success won with the Paris Critics, the young company became a Dramatic Centre in 1949. Because it was composed of Toulousains, having the Latin love of the theatre in their blood, the Grenier of Toulouse has been able to establish close links with its regional public who have rediscovered there a fellowship with the players. It is the best example of successful decentralization because it has provoked a type of acting which is its own and which could never have developed in Paris.

★   ★   ★

I have selected my own Eastern Dramatic Centre to show you the life of such a Centre. But first a word about the choice of repertoire, for which we may take all the Centres together, for with slight variations the five Centres select their plays from the same repertoire. Both because of their nature and public, the Centres choose mainly classical plays and the best works from contemporary playwrights. They attempt to make their audiences familiar both with the main dramatic schools and with the ideas as well as the new forms of theatre developed among leading modern writers. In the French classics Molière is the most popular, both because the spirit and style of his plays are within the understanding of the public and because the players are trained especially to perform his work. Marivaux, Beaumarchais and Musset, who are in the same tradition, are also frequently played, but Racine and Corneille much less so, partly because of the aristocratic form of French tragedy and the difficulty of finding actors capable of playing tragedy adequately.

Among foreign classics Shakespeare is most often produced, though it is difficult to find translations which are both faithful and dramatic. But the poetry of Shakespeare and the form of Elizabethan drama, which differs from that of French tragedy in that it follows a popular tradition, finds favour with a public who are generally more susceptible to emotion than the subtleties of psychology.

From contemporary drama the Centres play names such as Synge, Strindberg, Tchekhov, Pirandello, Lorca, Giraudoux, Claudel, Anouilh, Montherlant and Cocteau.

From these few names it will be seen that the Centres favour what is called *poetic realism*.

New plays, however, remain a problem for the Centres; on the one hand because in France as elsewhere there is a shortage of good manuscripts, and on the other because well-known authors prefer to give their plays to the directors of Paris theatres. And even the presentation of a good play by a little-known or unknown author raises numerous problems for the director of a Centre. His public, in general, is not sufficiently familiar with the art of our time. It is, equally, more sensitive than the Parisian public to religious, moral or political prejudices. Finally, the very fact that the Centre plays in a different town each night means that the critics have little influence on the success of a production. A bad criticism or an unfavourable welcome make themselves felt on the following production, not on the one being played at present, since the criticism is only read *after* the single performance has been given. The audience come instead to our productions on the draw of an author's name or a play already known. The solution of this difficult problem is without doubt the confidence which, over time, the public will have in each Centre, so that they come not to see such and such a play but *the* production of the Centre. Lectures, readings of new plays and so on can help the public so that they will not shy away from what they do not know. But as long as the repertoire of the Centres is not a creative one, if possible from regional authors, the work of the Centres will not reap its full harvest.

*   *   *

This, then, is the mission of the Centres, to found in each region a theatrical circle. So that this circle may be really fruitful, its activity should be associated with those writers who feel the need to escape from the Parisian monopoly.

Today, when it is primarily a question of restoring taste and feeling for the theatre, the Dramatic Centres must be

There is a school of acting at the Eastern Dramatic Centre as well as a professional company based on Strasbourg. Above, members at a rehearsal. Below, a production by Michel Saint-Denis of Jean Anouilh's *La Sauvage*.

The Eastern Dramatic Centre in Michel Saint-Denis' production of *Tessa*, by
Jean Giraudoux.

Actors believe in the future of the dramatic Centres. Michèle Manet and
Dominique Bernard in Marivaux's *La Surprise de l'Amour*.

The Centres continue the great tradition of acting, and Molière figures prominently in the repertoire. Here, a scene from *Le Misanthrope*.

closely dependent on a new public. I cannot think of a better definition for this public than the one Péguy pictured in his *Journal Vrai*: 'The challenging task to which we are harnessed is how to create again in this country a public, opposed to the continual debasement of soul or body, art or philosophy, against bourgeois vice, against demagogy, against sentimentalizing; how to build up a public which will once again be a sincere friend of truth, and beauty, a public of the people neither bourgeois nor plebean.'

A challenging task indeed, but just what paradoxically the Centres are now accomplishing. Who would have said, only ten years ago, that *Le Cid*, played before a public of railwaymen, would be one of the greatest successes of Jean Vilar? Who would have thought that Shakespeare, Molière and Lorca would be bigger box-office than the dreary hacks of the commercial theatre? And yet that is nevertheless what has happened. Not only has Jean Vilar in Paris been able to reach a public which had forgotten what a theatre was, but the Centres have now also incontestably succeeded in this same discovery of a new public. We find in industrial regions such as Montbéliard or the Moselle more and more workers crowding in to each performance (just as Jean Dasté now has a faithful public of miners in the region of St Etienne). At the same time, thanks to the educational authorities and the effective help of the Young Musicians of France (who on the musical side are doing the same work as ourselves) our public consists of a large majority of young people between sixteen and twenty-five, which augurs well for the future. And what joy, when playing for the first time in a new town where we may have given Molière or Marivaux before a thin house, when our audience increases at each performance until at the third or fourth we have to refuse admission.

But don't let us be too hasty in claiming victory; much still remains to be done. Although our prices are moderate (generally 400 francs, about 8*s.*, for orchestra stalls and often 150 francs or 3*s.* for workers' performances) and the

Association of Friends of the Centre organizes lectures and readings to facilitate our task, we still have to overcome prejudices against the theatre, considered as either a bourgeois entertainment or a literary affair reserved for 'cultured folk'; moreover the Centres, in so far as they are part of the life of the province, still lack in the eyes of many the traditional prestige of Paris productions.

*   *   *

The problems of authors and public have been mentioned, but that of actors is no less important. Except for the Grenier de Toulouse which, as I have explained, is a special case, the Centres recruit most of their actors in Paris, that is, periodically the directors have to go to Paris to hear auditions and engage players, either for a single production or more generally for a season. In fact, each Centre has a permanent company to which other actors may be added to suit the repertoire. Taking into account the modest finances of the Centres, along with the fact that it is impossible for actors working in the provinces to take part in films, television or, as a rule, radio programmes, members with talent tend to leave the Centres after a few years, and as the Centres act as a training ground for young actors it is difficult to keep experienced players. You must praise the unselfish sense of duty and love of theatre of those who stay on in very trying material and psychological conditions, with modest and often-forgotten thanks, in order that there should be a theatre for a public who would otherwise be deprived of it.

If the Centres are really going to become part of the life of the region, it is essential that the actors from Paris should gradually make way for local actors. That is why, in the organization of the Eastern Dramatic Centre, a High School of Dramatic Art has been established at Strasbourg. Its foundation was foreseen along with that of the Centre, but until 1954 economic circumstances delayed its opening. Today the *Direction des Arts et Lettres* and the Municipality of Strasbourg have built along the lines suggested by the architect Pierre Sonrel a building specially conceived for the Centre. This building consists of a theatre seating 800, with a stage projecting beyond the proscenium into the auditorium, and marks the culmination of research undertaken from the time of the Vieux-Colombier to the Old Vic. It possesses all the necessary quarters: a stage for rehearsing (a slightly reduced replica of the theatre stage), workshops for décor, carpentry, painting and costume designing, and numerous rooms for the courses of the school.

Thus the pupils, in the bosom of a theatre, have the chance of living in touch with artists and technicians in the course of their profession. The teaching they receive proceeds from the principles of the Vieux-Colombier which Jacques Copeau directed and from the experience I myself gained in the two schools that I directed: that of the London Theatre Studio, before the war, and then that of the Old Vic. In both of these there was the problem of rediscovering the art of acting which bad acting, naturalism and romanticism had lost for us. The potentialities of the modern methods of production are bound up with the existence of actors capable of playing according to new ideas, that is, of recreating, by the forcefulness of their acting, their power of human observation and their perfect mastery of body, a poetical climate arising from the dramatic transposition of reality. It was this necessity which forced Copeau and Dullin to open their schools near the theatres where they gave their productions.

The school consists both of actors and stage technicians. The acting course aims at developing the inventive powers and freedom of the actor. An important place is given to physical training and individual or choral improvisation, masked or otherwise, spoken or silent. But it is always dominated by the exigencies of performance, the reading of texts and the study of the main theatrical styles. Very special importance is attached to breathing, without which it is impossible to act freely and convincingly, and to voice production and the purity of diction, for the theatre lives by language—it is by his voice that the actor expresses his sensitivity and produces his greatest effect on the public.

The training of voice and body, however thorough it is, is of little use if they are not the servants of creative imagination. Far too frequently actors are satisfied with their 'gifts' and neglect to enlarge their imaginative and spiritual powers. That is why the masterpieces of all times and in all styles are studied by the pupils, along with the history of allied theatre arts.

The acting course lasts three years. At the end of the period the school presents in the villages of Alsace a performance in two parts, the first consisting of an entertainment of song, dance and mime, the second the staging of a French classic. This production completes the moulding of our pupils by giving them the indispensable experience of contact with the public.

At the present moment the school consists of two groups of student actors and one group of technicians, future stage managers, producers or designers. In all there are thirty-three pupils. They come principally from Alsace and Lorraine, but in the hope of escaping the dangers of 'provincialism' the school is open to the whole of France and to foreigners able to work in French. Already we have among us English, American, Spanish, Swiss and Israelite students as well as French. Under the direction of Suria Magito, French teachers work with instructors who were my colleagues in the Old Vic, Barbara Goodwin, John Blatchley, Pierre Lefevre and Jani Strasser. The studies are practically free and bursaries are provided if required. After leaving school the pupils try their fortunes in the vast world that is the theatre.

The organization of the Eastern Dramatic Centre consists of this school and a company of professional players: the *Comédie de l'Est*. I should like to complete this article with a description of a season in the life of the company.

We finished the 1953–1954 season in the month of July

and began rehearsals for the first two productions of the new season on 15th August. Our company had been divided into two, the one was to play a Marivaux programme consisting of *La Surprise de l'Amour* and *L'Epreuve*, the other Anouilh's *La Sauvage*. The rehearsals lasted about six weeks, the minimum time necessary if a production is to have some polish and not run risks on tour. We toured from the beginning of October until 15th December, giving fifty performances of each production. At the end of December we began the second part of the season, rehearsing, still with two companies, Shakespeare's *Romeo and Juliet* with one and with the other Mérimée's *Le Carrosse du Saint-Sacrement* and Jean Cocteau's *l'Antigone*. Again six weeks of rehearsals, then fifty performances of each production and that took us to the beginning of April. After a few days' rest we went ahead with the final part of the season's programme, giving a series of performances out of doors, a performance at the Strasbourg festival and several performances in Paris in the programme of the International Festival of Dramatic Art there. For this the two companies were combined to play *Romeo and Juliet* and Calderon's *L'Alcade de Zalaméa*. This third part of the season took us to the end of July, when the Centre closed for a month.

For the period from October to July the company consisted of never fewer than twenty actors, and had been up to thirty-six. All the décors and costumes of these productions had been designed by the two artists attached to the Centre for the season. They had all been made in our own workshops, and to give you some idea of the effort, during the month of January—for the two productions in the second part of the season—seventy costumes had to be made. From October until April 220 performances were given in eighty-two different towns.

Our Centre, originally established at Colmar, is now at Strasbourg. From that town we serve the whole region between the Rhine and a line from Lille to Reims, Dijon and Lyon. We also make occasional trips into Belgium and Switzerland.

Unlike the English system, where companies remain a week in each town, we are obliged to play at a different theatre every evening because the towns where we play are generally small. Some important towns such as Strasbourg, Mulhouse, Lille permit two or three consecutive perform-ances, very occasionally four.˙ This raises for us different problems of transport, for we play both in fully equipped theatres and in more modest ones. In a few cases there is no theatre at all, and we play in either a cinema or a hall, where equipment is lacking and stage hands are more willing than experienced. This constant changing of stages makes the task of décor extremely difficult. A décor has to be devised which can be adapted to a large stage without seeming small and to a small stage without being top-heavy. Often we have to construct two sets, a normal one and a miniature one. This solution, which is the best one for the audience, does not lighten the task of our stage hands and players. The latter, because dimensions vary each evening, have to try out afresh the production, and they have to adapt themselves at once to the size of the hall which may hold 300 or 1,500. As for stage hands, the scenery poses problems at each performance, to say nothing of the lighting.

These complex tasks demand immediate decisions, manual dexterity, a mentality which can easily adapt itself, and physical endurance for any task. Transport difficulties are a constant problem, as it is not always possible to arrange performances in towns near one another, and often long distances have to be travelled to the next theatre. This has forced us to send all our equipment by road; the sets and costumes travel in a lorry, the stage hands in a van, the actors by coach. It can be imagined what a tour is like under these tiring conditions where the slightest cold could quickly result in calamity.

There is, fortunately, the other side of the picture. The

welcome given by a new public, unspoilt by sophistication and snob appeal, discovering Shakespeare or Molière for the first time, is reward enough for all our efforts. The freshness of its reactions, the spell of silence in the hall, the excitement produced in these little towns on our arrival shows that we are on the right track. Our endeavours each evening bring their satisfaction when the little girl weeps at the death of Juliet or we meet the old fellow who never realized that the French language, thanks to Marivaux, possessed such richness and subtlety.

The French Dramatic Centres are still at a trial stage. Our task is a long uphill one. It is not possible to overcome, in a few years, time-honoured indifference. Encouragement is still needed, and support from the public authorities. Only when the Centres have gathered together their local strength, when each one is able to reflect a different tradition according to whether it is established at Strasbourg or Rennes, and when they are able to play regularly in Paris and exchange their productions with the best that Paris can offer, only then will they have won their exacting fight.

The Queen and the Rebels

A scene from the play by Ugo Betti
translated by Henry Reed

Ugo Betti (1892–1953) was a High Court judge who could not help reflecting what it must feel like to be unable to prove your innocence. And in a world run riot who could prove his innocence, who would be able to defend himself once caught up as the victim of an inhuman manhunt! With his intellectual brooding Betti sees that it is the individual who is always the condemned. So in The Queen and the Rebels *the rebels must sacrifice the Queen, but it is the common whore, who could never take anyone in for a moment to believe her other than what she is, who in the end finds she has no option but to go on play-acting . . . the rôle of her heart.*

[AMOS *has already risen; he speaks in the tones of a chancellor reading out an act.*
AMOS: The Accusation charges this woman with having concealed her identity, and falsified her papers.
ARGIA: Gentlemen! Please, please listen to me. I came up here . . .
AMOS: . . . with the intention of fleeing the country? Or to try to discover the whereabouts of your son? Yes, madam, we are fully informed about that also. Your son. [*His voice slightly rising.*] She is also accused of having formerly exercised a secret and illicit influence on the heads of the State, inducing them to enact factious and oppressive laws . . .

48

BIANTE: Oh, get on with it, Amos! You're cold, you've got no guts! You're just being cruel!

AMOS [*louder*]: ... of inciting massacre and persecution ...

ARGIA: But I have never done anything of the kind!

AMOS: ... of having fomented conspiracies aimed at undermining the authority of the State ...

ARGIA: But that's what you've done! And you blame it on the Queen! It's you who've been the sowers of discord.

AMOS [*louder*]: ... to the point of inducing a number of fanatics to take up arms against their country.

ARGIA: But I ...

AMOS: This woman is accused of having herself unloosed the present conflict; of having herself driven it to atrocious excesses. She herself summoned to this country foreign armed forces, herself lit the fires that now smoke from all points of the horizon, herself disfigured the dead along the roads ...

ARGIA: But I tell you I ...

AMOS: ... didn't know? Didn't want it?

ARGIA: I tell you that my hands ...

AMOS: Are clean? Is that it? That only shows how cunning you've been. It deprives you of extenuating circumstances, if there were any.

THE ENGINEER [*suddenly and violently*]: I was walking in the street one day: there was a cordon of soldiers; and they said to me: 'Not this way, the Queen will be coming down here.' I went round another way, and they told me: 'You can't come through here.' Everywhere I went, it was the same. Madam, you were always in the way.

ARGIA: Friends, friends, but I was there too, with you: on your side of the cordon, not the other.

A PEASANTWOMAN [*suddenly bursting into sobs*]: The shirt I washed for my son, he said it was shabby. He said the soup I cooked for him tasted nasty. And now they've told me that he's lying out there, in the fields, with his arms

D

wide open, covered with ants. It's all the Queen's fault.

ARGIA: You stone that woman now, only because you one day fawned on her!

A PEASANT [*violently*]: When our children are old enough to play games, they aren't allowed to play the same games as rich men's children. That's a terrible thing! That's what poisons their minds!

THE PEASANTWOMAN: My son hated the earthen crockery, he hated the smell of our home; he hated his own life!

THE WOMAN: It was your fault!

BIANTE: All of you! All of you! Bear witness, all of you!

THE ENGINEER: It was her fault.

MAUPA: It was her fault.

OTHERS: Hers. Hers, it was her fault.

BIANTE: And what about you? That porter over there! Are you the only one with nothing to say?   [*A silence.*

THE PORTER: Yes . . . everything she did . . . humiliated us.

ARGIA [*rebelliously, to* THE PORTER]: And who was waiting to teach humiliation and envy? Who was waiting to let your rancour loose?

AMOS [*with sudden intensity*]: You, the apex of privilege, the symbol of prerogative; you, the emblem of those distinctions from which humiliation and rivalry were born. Your whole celebrity is based and built upon inequality. It is in you that injustice is personified, it is in you that she finds her arrogant features, her scornful voice, her contemptuous answers, her sumptuous clothes, and her unsoiled hands. Your name of Queen is of itself enough to make men see that they are unequal: on one side vast revenues, on the other, vast burdens. You are the hook from which the great act of tyranny hangs. The world will be a less unhappy place when you have vanished from it.

ARGIA [*remains for a long moment with her head bent*]: Forgive me. I have been playacting a little; perhaps too much.

Now I will tell you the truth. I can prove that I am not
the Queen, and I can prove it at once. There is someone
here who can witness for me.

BIANTE: Who is it?

ARGIA: That man over there, your interpreter. Stop,
Raim, don't run away. He knows me very well indeed.
He knows I'm not a queen. I'm the sort of woman who
has to smile at lodging-house keepers, and traffic in pawn-
tickets.

RAIM [*comes forward slowly, in silence*]: There must be some
misunderstanding. This woman must be mad. I've
never seen her before in my life.

ARGIA: Look at me, Raim.

RAIM: I am looking at you. [*To* AMOS.] I've never seen
her before.

ARGIA [*turning to the others*]: My friend is frightened things
may have gone too far. Whether I'm the Queen or not,
or he's my friend or not, he's frightened that you have to
have a certain number of people to shoot, up here. He
just wants to stay alive, that's all.

RAIM: I knew you'd say that. But I must insist that I don't
know you.

ARGIA: Gentlemen! I and this man, who 'doesn't know'
me, kept each other warm all through one whole winter!

RAIM: Rubbish!

ARGIA: I came up here to look for him. There are people
here who saw us talking.

RAIM [*to the others*]: Of course they did. I tried to approach
her: because I thought she looked suspicious. I don't
know who she is. I'm sorry, madam, but I can't help you.
[*He moves away, disappearing among the others.* ARGIA
stands for a moment in silence.

ARGIA [*almost carelessly*]: Perhaps it's true. Perhaps that man
and I didn't ever know each other. But, even so, gentlemen, that doesn't give you the right to make stupid
mistakes. If you have to have a corpse to show people,
and tell everyone that the Queen's dead, you might at

least look for a corpse a bit more like her. You fools! I, the Queen? Is mine the voice of a Queen . . .? Has my life been the life of a Queen . . .? [*suddenly calling*] Raim! Raim! Call him back!

AMOS: I'd like to bet that your friend is far away by now. And that he's making for the mountains like a hare.

ARGIA [*bewildered*]: Gentlemen, there is someone else who can witness for me. There were two women travellers in this room: I . . . and another woman.

AMOS [*amiably*]: Yes. [*He makes a sign to one of the soldiers who at once goes out.*]

ARGIA: . . . a peasantwoman.

AMOS [*amiably*]: Yes. And where is she now?

ARGIA: She ran away. But she can't be far off. That woman . . . can tell you . . . that I'm not what you think. And you will have what you want, just the same. Send out and look for her.

AMOS: Up in the mountains?

ARGIA: Yes.

AMOS: All you can say of your witness, is that one is fleeing and the other has fled. [*A pause.*] Madam, we have a surprise for you. [*A pause.*] Your peasantwoman is here. She didn't get very far. Here she is.

> [*In a great silence,* THE QUEEN *appears, escorted by the soldier.* THE QUEEN, *pale, and rather still, looks round her.* AMOS *points to* ARGIA. THE QUEEN *comes forward to* ARGIA; *and speaks to her with a slight stammer.*]

THE QUEEN: Forgive me, my dear . . . it was all no use . . . I knew they'd have caught me . . . the moment I was so frightened of . . . arrived. . . . But I don't think . . . they've caught me in time . . . to hurt me. I managed to fool them . . . you know how . . . I prefer it . . . to be all over at once. Good-bye, my dearest friend. I was so afraid . . . but not so much, now. [*She sways, and sinks slowly to the ground.*]

BIANTE: What's going on?

ARGIA [*kneels down beside* THE QUEEN, *and takes her hand.*

After a while she looks up, and says, as though lost in thought]:
She carried poison with her. [*A pause.*] You have killed
her.

AMOS [*cutting her short*]: You are now completely without
accomplices. Say something, why don't you?

BIANTE [*shouting*]: You've no one left now!

AMOS: It's all over with you, your Majesty! Answer us!
You are the Queen!

ARGIA [*rises slowly*]: Not every eye shall look to the ground.
There shall still be someone to stand before you. Yes.
I am the Queen!

The Actor's Point of View

*

by Yvonne Mitchell

AN ACTOR becomes an actor either because he wants to exploit his own personality, or the very opposite. He may (and the majority of actors do) want to 'become' a lot of other people. His performance is usually a mixture of both—the portrayal of a character who is not himself, sieved through his own personality. He usually convinces himself that he is physically and mentally someone else, as a child will imagine himself a cowboy simply by being given a cowboy's hat. To the grown actor, the written word is his 'cowboy's hat'; and so it is the author who is the mainspring of the actor's imagination.

When an actor first reads a play he sees it as a whole, as a reader, producer, or critic will. Very soon he (rightly) gets submerged in his one part, and cannot see the wood for the tree. As the character he is portraying will be in the same state, unable to see anything except through his own eyes, he will be rightly interpreting the point of view of the character. I have read an essay by Brecht which seeks to alter this actor's point of view, so that the actor will in fact see the whole wood and 'comment' on his own particular 'tree'. If the theatre as a whole developed in this way, I think a different sort of person would want to act. Those people who are now lecturers, producers or critics by nature.

The actor as I know him does not want to comment, he he wants to 'be'. For myself, I want to be many different people. A slut, a siren, a prostitute, a romantic, a realist, a woman with a family, a childless woman . . . whoever I am I want to believe in. I will accept a part if at first glance I am willing to become that person; in fact if I feel no natural antipathy to her. Becoming her depends mostly on the other actors and my 'character's' response to theirs.

Strangely, one finds through experience that the audience is also a 'character' . . . part of the play; so that one's own part is never quite complete without them.

Audiences are a queer phenomenon. They become one person, play their part in unison, like the Greek character known as Chorus, and (in comedy) make the finished rhythm of a play. They are fresh in their reaction every night, but differ very little on one night or another.

Except for that extraordinary gathering at the first night of a play in London.

The chief trouble with the first night audience, as far as the actor is concerned, is that it cannot be made into a whole. Cannot, because it is not made up of mixable elements. Any other audience is composed of people who go to a play for very little reason except that they want to; who are therefore relaxed, and in a fit state to enjoy (or not) the fare that is presented to them.

But the people who take their seats at a London first night are more self-conscious. There is an amount of unrelaxed anxiety in the auditorium, an unfortunately infectious element: from people involved in the production (author, producer, backer, presenter), and from their friends and relatives. There are friends or relatives of the cast who are over-anxious to enjoy themselves, and show their approval, sometimes fatally, too soon after the curtain rises. There are well-dressed girls and women, anxious to be seen, who forget that they are there to watch, not to be watched. There are critics, anxious about what they will write about the piece. There are actors' agents, ticket agents, talent spotters . . . in fact 90 per cent. of the audience is there for a reason other than that of 'going to a play' . . . how can one turn such a group into a whole? They remain observers, and will not become participants. The unrelaxed atmosphere is caught by the actors, they play very often more forcedly than on any other night in their desire for response.

The actor cannot see the audience because the stage is lit and the auditorium is in darkness, but he can sense them, and assess them fairly accurately. He does not, on purpose, play any less well than his best every night, but as in tennis, he cannot get a continuous 'volley' if the other side are not sending the ball back. In a comedy it is the laughter which is sent back to him, in a drama it is a concentrated silence. Coughing is a sign of restlessness in the house, except in November when it is more often a sign of lung trouble.

That the auditorium is in darkness is an asset to the audience and to the actors. It is more difficult for most people to focus their attention if they can see the people around them, and for the actor it is awful. He instinctively pretends that the audience is not there, at the same time as needing it very badly. In fact his imagination is so divided that he can accept seeing a prompter at the side of the stage, because he is always there, but if a stage-hand or another actor watches one night from the side, within his view, he is 'put off' and loses concentration.

The amount an actor performs consciously or half-consciously is difficult to explain. Most actors perform in a mixture of both, which they are not themselves aware of. Some will say, 'Of course it's all conscious', others will protest that they perform instinctively; but I learnt for myself about the strange mixture in an early experience in rep: and I have since discovered that other actors are the same. I was playing the part of Tilly Slowboy in *The Cricket on the Hearth*. Tilly was a dim-witted nurse-maid, who so romantically loved the baby she was in charge of that she very often nearly dropped him because her thoughts were so deep in how much she loved him. In the third act I used to carry him up the stairs, trip, nearly drop him, and only just save his head from crashing on a stair in the nick of time. We played the play for a month. In the third week the producer's mother came to see the play, and said to me, 'I don't know how you manage that trip on the stairs. It's perfect.' Unfortunately I too then began to wonder how I did it, and for the next three days I muffed it. It simply didn't work. I went on the stage before each performance trying to find out which foot had been on which stair at which moment. I got it technically worked out at last, but it still didn't feel right, and the audience no longer laughed or gasped as I did it. After a couple more days I discovered the secret. That my thoughts should be on the baby and not on the execution of that particular technical feat, and as soon as I began to think only of the baby again, the technical feat accomplished itself. Of course I had from the first performance known that I tripped on the stairs and known that it was funny, but I had not consciously known exactly how and why. Leo McKern who was playing Guildernstern in *Hamlet* some time later at the Old Vic, told me that this semi-consciousness was bosh, and didn't apply to him at all. So I made a bet with him. I said, 'You know that as the Queen comes on, you sort of half flick your nose with your thumb every night?' 'Of course I know,' he said, 'I do it on purpose.' 'Now that I've brought it to your attention,' I challenged, 'see if you can do it again, so apparently instinctively.' 'Pooh!' he said. But I was right. For the next few nights, his instinctive gesture became 'an effect' and was awful. All he said to me afterwards was 'Damn you'. And Michael Redgrave once told me that someone had once praised the way he managed to fight Macduff, while backing up a flight of steps. 'The next night,' he said, 'I got my feet completely entangled.' This does not mean that an actor does not welcome praise. Of course he thrives on it. But praise of a whole, and not in detail. 'You say that line beautifully' is a way of ensuring that the actor will not say that line beautifully again. 'You're magnificent in that part' will suffice.

There is a rhyme I know which paraphrases all my feelings about acting . . . I don't know where it comes from:

'The centipede was happy quite
Until a toad in fun
Said, 'Pray, which leg comes after which?'
Which set her mind in such a fix
She lay distracted in a ditch
Considering how to run.'

I go to the theatre very often to see plays, and I still have the same reactions as I used to before I acted. I am never conscious of dressing-rooms, prompters, or the fact that there have been rehearsals, and that these people I now see in a seventeenth-century play have ever gone through the same motions in their everyday clothes and without beards or wigs. From the moment a curtain goes up I enjoy, or not, a play or performance without any reference to how it is done. I suppose because only what is happening on the stage now is relevant. I don't like going 'backstage' afterwards to see any actor I know, because being welcomed by someone in make-up and a dressing gown somehow destroys what I have seen; and also because, if I have been moved by a play, I will not yet have shaken off its impact, and the actor will have, so we shall be as at odds as if we were at a cocktail party where one of us was merry and the other sober. The actor shakes off the moods of a performance at the drop of the curtain; he sheds his 'character' as quickly as he sheds his coat. But don't misunderstand him. He does not put it on as lightly as he takes it off. Apart from the weeks of concentrated rehearsal for a part, he will spend between half an hour and two hours before every performance re-preparing himself for the character he plays.

Some people still regard the actor as 'a rogue and vagabond', my own father held the view that it was an immoral way of life, and that I would be a disgrace to the family. Some people admire, envy, or more often, dismiss the actor. In the small society of the theatre world he stands today rather low in importance. The producer (a modern innovation) stands first, the set-designer very often second, the actor third, and the playwright fourth. My own view is that the actor should stand second only to the playwright. They are all dependent on each other, and ultimately on the audience. The playwright cannot be judged except in performance. A literary play may mean very little when spoken or listened to, a play that has a meaning evident when played may read as a banal piece of work. But the play on paper is the starting point, and the basis of the work of the three others, and if any of these factors is inadequate it is likely that the final factor, the audience, will be inadequate too. As to the actor's relationship to each of these, he loves and respects the author. Not only because the author's work is the basis of his interpretation, but because in this case he has had a choice. What is offered to an actor by a management is a part in a play, and on this he says 'yes' or 'no'. So if he says 'yes' one assumes he is in sympathy with the play and the part. He is seldom offered the choice of a producer, designer or other actors. The actor's relationship with the producer varies from idolization to near murder. This will depend on how each feels the author's work should be carried out. The best relationship will come between a producer who is lucid about the play and has chosen that particular actor because his are the qualities needed, and an actor who is flexible and open to suggestion. The relationship between actor and designer is the producer's responsibility. He often has to make both sides compromise. The designer (of clothes or set) works visually, the actor physically, so a costume will offend a designer if it looks wrong, or will set an actor in revolt if he can't sit down in it. The actor will also be offended if the author's statements are not adhered to, whereas the designer feels he should be allowed to interpret more freely. There was a production of *Twelfth Night* in which soon after Maria had said that Malvolio was wearing yellow stockings, and stated that it was a colour detested by Olivia, the actress playing Olivia walked on the stage in a yellow dress. The producer and designer evidently didn't mind, but I'll bet the actress did.

Between actor and actor there is a rare sympathy. I have seldom met in practice the relationship one hears and reads about of actors trying to outdo each other by distracting, upstaging, or any other tricks. Actors get to know each other exceedingly well in a very short time. For some reason the only relationship I know of which is as unembarrassed is that which exists between children of the same family during their nursery years.

And finally, the actor and audience. They are a mysterious entity to him, he does not like to think of them as individuals but as a whole. I think if an actor saw the audience individually as they came into the foyer he would be as disappointed as the audience would probably be if they saw him arriving at the stage door. Both have a part to play which is not helped by any other contact than that which exists during the performance. I find that to be told someone 'important' is 'in front' is an irritation, and liable to put me off. The audience is a whole dark mass, partaking of an experience at the same time as the actor, and the less they know about each other apart from that experience, as far as I'm concerned, the better.

Stratford and Shakespearian Production

*

by T. C. Worsley

THEATRICALLY, the post-war period in England has been marked by what almost amounts to a re-discovery of Shakespeare, and I suppose it is certainly safe to say that at no period (at least since his own) have so many of his countrymen taken pleasure in the experience of seeing his plays performed. Doubtless an earlier generation read them as assiduously, if not more so. But the stage versions which they witnessed from time to time were only truncated and re-arranged adaptations of the actual plays. The eighteenth century, with its audacious and self-confident belief in its own taste, altered the texts whole-heartedly and unscrupulously in the interests of its idea of literary good manners; and the nineteenth, suppressing the whole of many, and large parts of the others, in the interests of its own prudery, presented a small repertoire of the 'inoffensive' plays as vehicles for their actor-managers.

It is our boast (posterity may, of course, see it in another light) that we have rescued the texts from the manipulators and bowdlerizers, and have rescued them, too, from the readers and even the scholars: or, rather, that we have used the scholars to help us to realize the texts on the stage instead of in the study. Actually, of course, we seldom see the whole of a Shakespeare play even now: they run too long for our theatre conventions. But what we do see is what Shakespeare wrote, and what we aim at is to achieve the playwright's original intentions in so far as we can

61

discern them. When cuts are necessary, they are made only because time insists, and even then they are made as far as possible only to further dramatic unity. Yet this reformation would only be of academic or pedantic import-ance if it were not paralleled by an intense revival of interest among audiences, who flock to Shakespeare now as to almost no other dramatist. The situation at Stratford may be taken as the very symbol of this. Between the wars, although there was usually a fine company maintaining a reasonably high standard at Stratford, it was always possible to drop in and find a seat in the large Memorial Theatre. But in the last five years the theatre could have been sold out for the whole season almost before the season began, and only a deliberate policy leaves a few of the cheaper seats to be booked on the day of performance itself.

The reasons for this revival of interest would be com-plicated to analyse and perhaps tedious too. But very broadly one can say that what has happened is this: a move-ment deriving from William Poel and the Elizabethan stage society in the 'nineties, and developed by Granville Barker in the nineteen-tens, directed at rediscovering the texts themselves, has met a generation of remarkable actors and actresses who have been as much interested in the plays as wholes as in the parts for which they might prove vehicles. And between the two has been conceived the discovery that Shakespeare, acted in full, provides the most complete theatrical pleasure available in our native repertoire. If the movement goes on, the worst efforts of the pedants and the pedagogues will be defeated; not even the examination-setters themselves will be able to stifle the truth that Shakespeare is a dramatist, and is there to be enjoyed!

This change of taste coincides not only with a general raising of our educational levels but also with a welcome raising of theatrical standards. Between the wars—and this itself was a legacy of the Edwardian period—the leading actors and actresses became 'leading' by virtue of their skill in light comedy and romance. To put it crudely, Sir Gerald du Maurier, effortlessly easy and polished, natural and realistic, set the tone to which a whole generation of acting aspired. But now once more we judge our actors and actresses as 'leading' by their ability to match the great classical, and above all, the Shakespearian rôles. We owe this reversal almost entirely to the work of one man, Sir John Gielgud. Sir John, like most of his contemporaries was trained in that school of Shakespeare, the Old Vic, where throughout the period Miss Lilian Bayliss kept the flag flying in spite of a thousand difficulties. But it was Sir John (deriving his practice largely from Granville Barker) who first persuaded the general theatre-going public between the wars that there was nothing esoteric about Shakespeare: who, to put it another way, replanted the flag of Shakespeare in the commercial West End. Of course it was his great gifts as an actor that worked the trick, just as it is the star qualities which have enabled Sir Laurence Olivier, Michael Redgrave, Peggy Ashcroft and the others to follow in his footsteps. But the point is that he—and they—have not been content merely to exploit their personal qualities; they have preferred to use them as only one element, though a very important one, in this fresh treatment of the plays, which has brought scholarship to bear on the texts, historical imagination on the décor, teamwork from the whole company in the acting, and so brought the plays alive for us in a new way.

This success was consolidated in the famous Old Vic seasons, just after the war, when the Waterloo Road building was still demolished and the New Theatre housed a glittering company led by Sir Laurence Olivier and Sir Ralph Richardson. But this was a sort of super West End Old Vic which wouldn't in the nature of our present theatrical organization be a permanency. And it was a yet younger generation, led by Mr Anthony Quayle, who set out to make a permanency of this tradition and decided to establish it at the most appropriate of all places for it, Stratford. Sir Barry Jackson who was then in charge there welcomed the invasion, and the next year indeed handed over complete command to Mr Quayle who had, at the first charge, made a brilliant success of the venture. Previously Stratford (although it seems unfair when you look at the names of the admirable actors and producers who worked there) had remained, as a season, curiously provincial. It was, if the least important for the long run, a most important achievement for the short, that Mr Quayle at a clap made it fashionable. The importance of this resided simply in the fact that a theatre must pay its way, and the Memorial Theatre is that rarity in our world, a classical theatre that is unsubsidized. But the interesting thing is that it became fashionable not by calculated glamourization—Mr Quayle's first season offered no great 'star' names. What Mr Quayle did was merely to apply the new principles of Shakespearian production to Stratford too. The productions were set and dressed by the more adventurous of our young designers, and were directed by the younger followers of Mr Tyrone Guthrie, who had made something of a speciality of producing on the grand scale (essential on that large wide stage) and who himself undertook some of the earlier productions. These first seasons had all the excitement of an experiment about them, zest, youth and fire; and the public responded.

Within two years Mr Quayle had established Stratford as *the* centre of Shakespearian production, and once that was done it was possible to maintain it as such. With its reputation remade, any of the leading actors and actresses would be prepared to make the financial sacrifices necessary to play a season there for the good of their reputations. Some of the highlights of the last seven years will be long remembered. Mr Peter Brook's production of *Measure for Measure*, for instance, brought this dark and difficult play alive for a generation which had hardly had the chance of seeing the play before. In the same season Sir John Gielgud, who had played Angelo in that play, gave us a most memorable, indeed in my opinion a very great, Lear, with Peggy

Stratford: Michael Benthall's production of *The Tempest*, with an imaginative decor by Loudon Sainthill.

Othello tours Australia and New Zealand in a production by Anthony Quayle, with decor by Tanya Moiseiwitsch. Anthony Quayle plays Othello and Barbara Jefford Desdemona. Extreme right, Leo McKern as Iago.

Glen Byam Shaw's production at Stratford of *Anthony and Cleopatra*. Decor by Motley. With Peggy Ashcroft as Cleopatra and Marius Goring as Caesar. This production was seen in London and on the Continent.

Above: *All's Well that Ends Well* Stratford production by Noel William with decor by Mariano Andreu. Below: Glen Byam Shaw's production of *Troilus and Cressida* with decor by Malcolm Pride. Heads on left: top, Laurence Harvey as Troilus bottom, Leo McKern as Ullysses. Bernard Kay and Muriel Pavlow play Diomede and Cressida on stage.

Ashcroft as his Cordelia. Stratford marked Coronation Year with an ambitious venture, the full impact and importance of which was only really felt when it was over. This was to play in succession the four historical plays which follow chronologically on one another, *Richard II*, the two parts of *Henry IV* and *Henry V*. As this chronicle unfolded itself, especially to those who were seeing the plays on successive nights, the grandeur and scope of this four-part work became fully manifest perhaps for the first time. Finally no one who saw it will forget Mr Glen Byam Shaw's superb production of *Antony and Cleopatra* two seasons later, in which Miss Peggy Ashcroft and Mr Michael Redgrave triumphed as the protagonists.

These are only a few of the memorable achievements of Stratford, but the importance of the rebirth of Stratford does not lie only in its highlights. The important thing is that it should provide, there of all places, the finest Shakespearian production available. The Stratford seasons now set a standard (a standard which, goodness knows, it is difficult to maintain) which has an influence on the whole field. It is safe to say that had it not been for Stratford's example, the level of productions at the Bristol Old Vic, the Birmingham Repertory, and even the Old Vic itself, would not have been so high.

But no problem in art is ever solved, and, striking though the achievement has been when we look back on it, certain dissatisfactions with the direction which Shakespearian production is now taking are also beginning to express themselves. The older generation complain that the poetry of Shakespeare is too often sacrificed to the production. There is too much truth in this. The Guthrie school of production, to which most of the younger producers belong or have belonged, brilliantly inventive and imaginative as it is, has the besetting sin of overdoing everything. One of the assumptions behind it seems to have been that Shakespeare, at least as he had been presented in the past, was boring, and that they were justified in almost any antics

E

which would make it 'exciting'. Above all (since this
school derived in part from ballet) they seemed to be
frightened of its becoming static, and 'movement' became
one of their great watchwords. In other words they couldn't
trust the verse to make its own effect, but were always
trying to illustrate it by invented action. The result has
been to take the poetry out of the centre, and distract the
attention of the audience by paralleling the speech with
(more or less) significant business and movement. A
complementary fault has been to over-dress, and to over-
elaborate the whole visual side of their productions, again
at the expense of the aural.

These are, of course, remediable faults, and they only hint
at the real problem lying behind. This problem is inherent
in the fact that we are condemned to playing Shakespeare
on a kind of stage—the picture frame stage—for which
his work was not intended. He wrote for an open stage
with a large platform out into the auditorium and the
audience sitting round three sides of it. This type of theatre
invited a really very different kind of illusion, and worked
by a quite different set of conventions, from those which
the picture stage invokes. And this difference has set
producers two main technical problems, for one of which
we have found a good compromise solution, while the
other has barely been tackled yet. When we do tackle it
we may have some idea of the way in which Shakespearian
production is likely to move in the future.

The first problem was that the Elizabethan stage allowed
Shakespeare to use what we now think of as a cinemato-
graphic technique passing instantaneously from one place
to another and jumping gaps of time as well as of place
without these changes being emphasized by anything but
the words. But the picture stage conventions seemed to
demand something more 'real'; these movements of time
and place had to be marked visually as well as aurally.
The result was that, with frequent scene changes and
intervals to mark lapses of time, not only did the plays

become inordinately long, but the dramatic rhythm and pace were completely lost.

To restore these has been the great technical achievement of our new approach to Shakespeare, and the permanent or semi-permanent set has been the technical means of doing it. Audiences are now so accustomed to these impressionistic structures that they hardly remember that there was ever any other way of mounting Shakespeare. We take in our stride now this transformation of the picture frame theatre; we accept the structures, whether left bare for our imaginations to work on, or transformed by clever lighting or decked out with a few evocative properties which transfer the stage in a moment from an interior to an exterior, from a closet to an arbour or a throne room. And by accepting this illusion, we have regained the dramatic rhythm. But I think a further reason why the problem of the poetry and of verse-speaking has been neglected is that producers have been so intent on solving this problem of restoring the pace and on trying to improve on and develop the technical solutions offered, that they have let the problem of the verse go by the board. And that is the problem that now demands to be solved.

Many Shakespearian producers and actors are now agreed that this problem can be solved satisfactorily only by some further transformation of the picture frame stage. Mr Tyrone Guthrie, who is an ardent supporter of this view, has made some experiments (especially in Canada) with a full platform stage of the Elizabethan kind, and actors who have performed there, with the audience on three sides of them, report that there is a quite different and very exciting sense of intimacy and intercommunication between actors and audience under these conditions. On the picture frame stage the actors are cut off by the footlights from the audience; they have to 'project themselves' across it, and draw the audience into their removed illusion. On the deep platform stage they are in among the audience, sharing—so the argument runs—their feelings and reactions with a warm immediacy. And in those conditions—they assert—the verse 'works' more potently and effectively. If the advantages of this method of production prove overwhelming—and it begins to look as if they will—then another even more difficult technical problem will face producers. They will have to find some compromise as effective as the permanent set has been in its way to add this further transformation. For, of course, it is not practicable to rebuild all our playhouses to suit this theory (which may itself in the course of time give way to yet another). The permanent set allows the action to be shuffled to and fro with the same rapidity as did the Elizabethan stage. To discover some illusory way of giving us the same sort of satisfaction that the platform stage offers would seem to be the next technical step to be taken in Shakespearian production.

The Bristol Old Vic

*

by John Moody

THE Bristol Old Vic Company at the Theatre Royal holds a unique position in the theatre of this country, due largely to the history of its development. It may well prove to be the pilot for a great revival of the theatre outside London.

The theatre, itself the oldest working theatre in the country, was built in 1766. For many years it was the most prosperous in the provinces, and it was no uncommon sight to see over a hundred carriages at its doors. Almost every actor and actress of note played there, except David Garrick, who, however wrote the prologue for the opening, and is said to have pronounced it to be the most complete theatre for its dimensions in Europe. Sarah Siddons was a member of the stock company between 1779 and 1781. But by 1939 its fortunes had declined so far that it was supporting only the lowest forms of variety and pantomime. New and larger theatres had been built in Bristol which housed distinguished touring companies, the Little Theatre was playing a repertory of popular West End successes, and it seemed as though the Royal's honourable career was finished. When in 1942 it was doomed to become a warehouse, a small body of local citizens who could not bear to see this lovely building so dishonoured between them raised capital towards buying the fabric. At the same time they approached the Arts Council of Great Britain (or C.E.M.A. as it then was) to see if they could help to complete the purchase and restore the building. Lord Keynes, C.E.M.A.'s chairman, at once grasped the possibilities of the situation: this might become the first 'national' theatre building supported by the Exchequer. So C.E.M.A. took a lease and paid for the restoration of the building, which now, with its beautifully restored Georgian green paint and gilding, attracts many visitors who come to see the building alone even when there is no play on.

In 1945 it was decided to ask the Old Vic, who had run a very successful company at the Playhouse in Liverpool, to run a similar company at the Theatre Royal. Then was formed one of the most interesting features of its development, its management committee. This was formed of two members of the Arts Council, two members of the Old Vic Trust, and an independent chairman. In 1949, when the Arts Council had suddenly been faced with spending another £20,000 on the building to comply with new fire regulations, they approached Bristol Corporation for help. The corporation, who felt that the company had become a real asset to Bristol, came forward with an annual grant towards the maintenance of the building and its equipment, and two of the councillors joined the management committee. The commercial theatre has always understood the importance of the proper administration and finance of the bricks and mortar, and the artistic theatre has always understood the importance of a clearly defined artistic policy: but seldom in this country have the two worked together. Here, at last, were the experts in real estate and in art uniting for the good of the drama. Only where there is a supporting framework for it can the art of the drama develop in these difficult times. Bristol has shown a way of doing it and other great cities are following its example.

Continental countries have an advantage over us in that the art of the drama traditionally is taken seriously and enjoyed by all lines of life. This is possible because it has been subsidized, first in the court theatres and later in the municipal and national theatres. In this country there has been a tendency to associate the serious theatre only with the social or intellectual snob. The ordinary man in the street, because he cannot afford unsubsidized theatre prices, has grown accustomed to getting his entertainment from the films, with an occasional 'outing' to a commercial 'show', and now from television. This position has got to be remedied by increasing the income of the theatre from outside sources such as subsidies, or perhaps by liaison with television, also by keeping serious drama in touch with a far wider and livelier public. The difficulty is to find plays which have a wide enough appeal: plays of action rather than of introspection; of movement and colour rather than in the domestic four walls; and in the language and idiom of our own day.

The artistic policy of the Bristol Old Vic has been founded not unnaturally on that of the parent company in London, and has been predominantly classical. But it has always been felt that such a company should be concerned not only with performing past classics, but with creating future ones. This is becoming increasingly important in a time when the financial conditions in the London theatre are fast becoming like those of New York: there it is almost impossible to try out a production of a new play unless it is a certain winner with a star cast.

The season's programme for 1954-5 may give a little idea of the company's present aims. The great classics were represented by Shakespeare's *Much Ado about Nothing*, *The Merchant of Venice* and *The Winter's Tale*. To open the season we chose a lesser eighteenth century classic, Holcroft's *The Road to Ruin*. This was a piece of the period of the theatre building which was just being reopened after redecoration and regilding. At moments in the play the fusion of the setting and building made it hard to divide the auditorium from the stage picture. This was followed by a contemporary setting of a very contemporary play, *Marching Song*, in a production which served to prove that its author John Whiting can claim a devoted and enthusiastic audience in Bristol as well as in London. Later, Peter

Ustinov's *No Sign of the Dove* made the success it ought to have made in London. Bristol with less money and only repertory casting can sometimes offer a good author a better second showing of a play which London theatre mischances have killed.

This season saw the first production in this country of Arthur Miller's *The Crucible*, an American play, set in seventeenth century Salem yet dealing with the very topical menace of the hysteria of witch-hunting. After *The Two Bouquets* at Christmas followed the first performance of *Image in the Sun* by the successful novelist Howard Clewes. The drawing of serious writers from other realms of literature into the theatre is most important for its future. As a more recent classic and example of French theatre, *The Enchanted* by Giraudoux has proved a happy choice. Denis Johnston's *The Golden Cuckoo*, a subtly quixotic comedy, made its appeal mostly to the younger playgoers and the young in heart. The last two plays of the season were Eliot's *The Confidential Clerk*, the only West End success we have put on this season, and a comedy of ideas, *You and Your Wife*, by Denis Cannan, whose *Captain Carvallo* was first put on here before Sir Laurence Olivier took it to the St James's Theatre.

Our basic acting company is limited by financial considerations to only twelve, far too small for a classical company. Other actors have to be engaged by the play. We hope that one day means will be found to engage a full company for the whole season, and so to give the actors the necessary security and time to develop as a team on the same lines as the well-known continental companies. This will also mean that we might one day be able to run in true repertory like the Old Vic and Stratford. In this way performances of worth-while, but less popular, plays can be spread over a much longer period and their reputation built up without so much loss. This might help new authors. It would also make possible some of the visits abroad which we are asked to do, but which now are nearly always impossible owing to the fixed run-of-the-play system.

One more interesting development must be mentioned. The Bristol Old Vic runs a lively drama school recently housed in excellent new premises. The accent is above all on the students having the right physique, and its proper development for creative expression. There are many intelligent actors today, but few who have the physical equipment for great acting. There is also in Bristol University the first department of drama in this country. The school, the university and the theatre are linked in each other's affairs on the artistic and administrative levels, and students come in from all over the world. With the joint efforts of physical (and vocal) development, historical research, a beautifully equipped drama studio and a practising theatre, who knows but that this may not prove a cradle and a nursery for many much-needed new ideas in playwriting and presentation to liven up the theatre.

Playgoing over Here and over There

*

by Alan Dent

PLAYGOING in New York has a kind of tension about it which we very seldom feel in London, even at a first night. I did six weeks of active playgoing on Broadway in the winter of 1953, and it is not perhaps a long enough period on which to form any judgment of any value. But the general first impression that abides is that, whereas the London playgoers hope to be pleased, or are even determined to be pleased, the New York playgoers have a defiant air which seems to say: 'Please us if you can—we shall not be very demonstrative either way.' Nor are they!

One must and should, of course, differentiate between the first-night audience and that of any other night. The difference is as great in New York as it is in London. The tension of playgoing at a New York first night is acute and extreme, whereas in London—unless on some quite exceptional occasion—it may be said to be merely existent and perceptible: something which may at least be *called* tension.

One of my New York first nights was that of a spectacular revue of English origin, but with many favourite American performers supporting our own ineffable Hermione Gingold. From the first appearance of that witty witch everything went triumphantly. Even the dramatic critics were seen to beam, and there was a general rapture in the air the like of which I had not sensed after any revue since the heyday of Charles Cochran at the London Pavilion. But even so, as I remember the occasion, there were not innumerable curtain-calls at the end. The tendency in New York is rather towards keeping the curtain up for quite a time to allow the assembled actors and the audience—loath apparently to dis-assemble itself—to beam at one another and simply babble with enjoyment.

At a disastrous first night, on the other hand, the tendency is diametrically opposite. I attended the first performance on Broadway of a light comedy from the French, for three characters only and set on a desert island. It had run for more than three years in Paris, and for more than two in London. My diary records what happened: 'A hapless first showing. The audience at the end could not leave the theatre quickly enough. This, I learn, is their usual behaviour at a disastrous first night. They rush to the exits before the actors have finished their perfunctory bows. This ought to be a privilege accorded only to the dramatic critics!'

Was it ever thus? It is extraordinarily difficult to find out. Our greatest actor of the mid-nineteenth century, Macready, has passages in his journal of the greatest relevance and quotability. Of his very first visit to New York in 1826, when he had already a high reputation in London though still in his early thirties, he has written: 'It was my practice never to undervalue my audiences; and, though I often found them in America less sensitive and more phlegmatic than those at home, I wrestled with the tendency to yield to their apparent want of sympathy, and by acting determinedly to the character I had to represent, my hearers gradually kindled into excitement.'

Macready dutifully recorded an episode which is going to have no comment from me whatsoever though it is certainly not uninteresting: 'The house was crowded, and my reception all I could desire. The only occurrence to remind my wife and sister, who occupied a private box, that they were not in an English theatre was the rough treatment of a black woman, who by some mistake had got into the pit, and for a length of time was hustled about from one to another amidst shouts of laughter from the white spectators, until at last she got into a corner, and, nestling down there, was suffered to remain unmolested during the remainder of the evening. No coloured person was at that time allowed to sit either in the boxes or pit.'

For the rest, Macready has disappointingly little to say about his actual reception or about the audience's general atmosphere: 'My performances being limited to the repetition of the characters in which I had gained reputation at home, gave occasion to little remark. The houses were nightly crowded, my emoluments were most satisfactory, and thus three weeks passed away agreeably enough.'

Only a year earlier in the very same theatre another great visitor from England, Edmund Kean, had known exactly how hostile a New York audience could be. Though a huge audience filled the theatre, Kean, playing King Richard III, might just as well have stayed at home. Not a single. word that he spoke could be heard above the noise of hisses and counter-cheers which was kept up unremittingly throughout the action of the play. But the reason for this had nothing to do with Shakespeare or the quality of Kean's acting. The hiss was a moral hiss: Kean had been the subject of a divorce-court scandal in the English law-courts, and he had in point of fact been hounded off the London stage to the American one, where he vainly hoped to find sanctuary and sympathy.

Macready himself was later to know the humiliation of hisses and boos and even worse from a New York audience. This was at the height of his rivalry with the American tragedian, Edwin Forrest, in the year 1849, just two years before Macready retired from the stage altogether. With an extraordinary mixture of honesty and humourlessness the English tragedian describes with monumental dignity everything as it exactly happened: 'They would not let me speak. They hung out placards—"You have been proved a liar," etc., flung a rotten egg close to me. I pointed it to the audience and smiled with contempt, persisting in my endeavour to be heard. I could not have been less than a quarter of an hour on the stage altogether, with perfect sangfroid and good humour, reposing in the consciousness of my own truth. At last there was nothing for it, and I said "Go on," and the play, *Macbeth*, proceeded in dumb show, I hurrying the players on. Copper cents were thrown, some striking me, four or five eggs, a great many apples, nearly—if not quite—a peck of potatoes, lemons, pieces of wood, and a bottle of asafoetida which splashed my own dress, smelling, of course, most horribly.' This was in the first act alone. Later the audience took to tearing up the chairs and throwing them into the orchestra and on to the stage.

But all this was the behaviour of a maddened audience out of hand. In the same bad old days it could get just as much out of hand in London. It is the normal behaviour of the normal audience which should be our study. When a later and greater American tragedian, Edwin Booth, came to London in 1880 he met at first with something with which even Macready's sangfroid and contemptuous smile could not cope. This was sheer frigidity of a sort we meet with only on Broadway today. Three days after his opening in *Hamlet* we find Booth writing in a letter to a friend: 'They tell me my success is *great* and all that. But the Press damns me with faint praise—the audiences are cold and dead, truly British.' Americans in London growled of 'insular spleen'. This annoyed and embarrassed Booth, who wrote to another friend: 'I think the *gush* of my countrymen has here injured me somewhat. There's no restraining the eagle when he feels like screeching, and he *scroched* too much for me.'

Booth, it is clear, had a humour which was lacking in Macready. He did not, it is true, show much humour or even much gratitude when Irving—three months after his unhappy season had begun—invited him to the Lyceum to exchange with Irving the great rôles of Iago and Othello.

Irving's motives were variously interpreted by friends on
both sides. Whatever they were, Irving was the one who
risked most, and his timely invitation was a life-saver to
Booth. Ellen Terry in her autobiography wrote: 'I cannot
be sure that Booth's pride was not more hurt by this
magnificent hospitality than it ever could have been by
disaster. It is always more difficult to *receive* than to *give*.
Few people thought of this, I suppose. I did, because I
could imagine Henry Irving in America in the same situation—accepting the hospitality of Booth. Would not he,
too, have been melancholy, quiet, unassertive, *almost* as
uninteresting and uninterested as Booth was?' Fair-minded
as well as feminine of Ellen Terry.

She herself notes one particular instance of the different
perceptiveness of the New York as compared to the London
audience, and its different manner of expressing itself. She
is writing of her first appearance with Irving in *Charles I*
in which she played Queen Henrietta Maria: 'I could not
command myself. I played badly and cried too much in
the last act. But the people liked me, and they liked the
play, perhaps because it was historical; and of history the
Americans are passionately fond. The audience took many
points which had been ignored in London. I had always
thought Henry as Charles I most moving when he made
that involuntary effort to kneel to his subject, Moray. But
the Lyceum audiences never seemed to notice it. In New
York the audience burst out into the most sympathetic
spontaneous applause that I have ever heard in a theatre.'
That was in the year 1883.

But nowadays no audience, on either side of the Atlantic,
would ever break into applause at a serious play before the
fall of the curtain. Other times, other manners—but not
necessarily better manners! The New Yorkers never boo
or hiss nowadays, and think it unmannerly of us to do so.
The Londoners, on the other hand, never run away *en
masse* at the last curtain-fall, leaving the actors unapplauded;
and they think it unmannerly of the Americans to do so.

On the one hand, a case can be made out for sounds of disapproval; on the other, a case can be made out for the silence of disapproval. The Englishman, as I began by saying, goes hoping to be pleased; the American goes expecting to be displeased. We are so very alike in one sense, and so very different in another.

There is the ultimate and most paradoxical point of all, that our behaviour at the theatre is not characteristic of us as a nation—and that neither is theirs. The distinguished drama critic of the *New York Times* remarked to me in London the other day: 'Why is it that you English, who are supposed to be so cool and phlegmatic, seem to relax and enjoy yourself so much at the theatre?' And I could only reply with another question: 'Why is it that you Americans, who are supposed to be so warm and demonstrative, sit in the theatre in a state of tension and as often as not appear relieved and delighted to pass out into Broadway again?'

The Irish Theatre

a decline and perhaps, in the end, a fall

*

by Gerard Fay

IN ITS VERY simplest terms a theatre consists of actors, dramatists and audience. Some auxiliary troops come into it as well, such as producers, technicians, designers— even critics. But actor, dramatist, spectator are the three who make the theatre possible. When the theatre in question is aiming to be a national one, some new complexities arrive; when it is an Irish National Theatre, paradox piles on complexity and definition itself becomes a dangerous venture.

The earliest definition of an Irish National Theatre that I have found was written by my father in *The United Irishman* in 1901:

My notion . . . is that it ought to be the nursery of an Irish dramatic literature which, while making a world-wide appeal, would see life through Irish eyes. For myself, I must say that I cannot conceive it possible to achieve this except through the medium of the Irish language.

Later in the same year Edward Martyn published his *Plea for a National Theatre in Ireland,* which was an ingenious attempt to get money from the government on the ground that a school of acting should come under the Department of Technical Instruction. But a British government fifty-five years ago was in no danger of falling for that sort of thing. There was nothing in common between the two proposals, yet they both had the same aim of establishing what might come to be recognized as an Irish Theatre.

After some false starts and misunderstandings the theatre was established and flourished under the name of the Abbey. It reached a climax in the 'twenties when the plays of Sean O'Casey burst upon Dublin audiences which had become accustomed to the Abbey as a half-dead repertory theatre from which no new ideas were to be expected. Whether there is now, or will long remain, such a thing as 'the Irish theatre' is questionable. There is no reason why it should not fade away as quickly as it grew, for it was created by conditions which have now been removed, and was part of Ireland's answer to questions which are no longer worth asking.

There is no reason why a small country suffering from anaemia of the political system, as Republican Ireland does, and willingly surrendering much of its intellectual freedom to a dominant Church, should be capable of steadily supplying the English-speaking world with plays of some importance written in a purely Irish mood and language. I have a book on the Irish theatre which runs to 500 pages; the period 1900–1945 occupies only four of them. I have another which, in well over 200 pages, does not get any farther than 1720. I can produce a list of dramatists much longer than the familiar Congreve-Farquhar-Goldsmith-Sheridan-Wilde-Shaw series which proves that there were Irishmen well able to write excellent plays before 1900. Yet I should exaggerate if I said that these men and their plays could be called an Irish theatre.

The early history of the stage in Ireland showed it as a mere provincial branch of London although it built its own theatres and bred its own actors. Most important, it had a lively audience, so that when there seemed a chance of establishing a really Irish theatre there was some foundation to work on. It was not necessary to teach people to go to the theatre; the lesson that had to be taught was that the acting talent of Irish men and women might be

F

turned to something more useful than supplying comic relief in English melodrama.

An audience could be found; there was a distant prospect of actors being trained. But where were the dramatists? They were either wallowing in Anglo-American commercialism or straying after Ibsen on lines more likely to lead to a municipal than a national theatre. What pulled them together was the discovery that a company of Irish players, or at least the very raw material for such a company, was struggling for existence and that what it lacked was an Irish play or two to work on. The Irish literary theatre was limping towards its end; Irish plays by Moore, Martyn and Yeats had been murdered by Benson and other English players. There seemed no point in going on, but Yeats and George Russell were struck by some quality in the acting of the brothers Fay, something instinctively right, though one brother was self-taught and the other had experience only with crude English travelling companies. The actors and the dramatists found each other; arguing about who found whom first is no more profitable than taking sides between Sherpa and Sahib in the debate about who first stepped on to the summit of Everest.

It was true that an audience could be found. It was not easy to find the right audience. Dubliners were good theatre-goers sixty years ago. The fashionable thing was to be seated in the dress circle of the Gaiety when some decent English company was visiting; with luck the Lord Lieutenant and his lady might attend and make it a gala. Anyway, it was done to be seen there; it was not done to be seen at the Queen's (the house that now holds the Abbey as refugee from the fire of 1951), because there you could never be sure that some Irish melodrama might not be on, in which there would be disrespectful references to Britain, or even to Her Majesty. Though the audiences at both theatres were largely Irish they were not likely to support a national theatre in which Irish matters were taken seriously.

Young men and women were beginning to take up the

Irish language, Irish games, Irish arts and crafts, all as part of the movement towards Irish independence. Nothing could have been easier than for the Irish theatre to jump on the same bandwagon and it was urged to do so. But there were several reasons why it had to limp along behind. First, the money to build the Abbey had come from Miss Horniman, an Englishwoman who would have nothing to do with Irish nationalism and who despised most of the Irish except Yeats and Lady Gregory. Secondly, Yeats wanted to use the theatre as a centre of poetic-dramatic revival in which he was a natural leader. He would not be tied down to motives pressed on him from the outside. Therefore the early interest shown in the national theatre by Arthur Griffith and Maude Gonne, both extreme nationalists preparing to use force against Britain, turned first to caution then to outright opposition.

The result was that the Abbey was treated with suspicion by the national leaders and never aroused much enthusiasm among the chief politicians of free Ireland, though from the moment an Irish government was set up the Abbey became in the fullest sense a national theatre, subsidized by the State.

Just after the subsidy came a slight burst of activity caused by the eruption of Sean O'Casey, but otherwise the Irish theatre began to die almost as soon as Ireland got self-government. There was joy at the arrival of a new major dramatist who quickly qualified for a place beside Synge by writing a play which caused riots and fisticuffs in the Abbey. Within a few years joy turned to no more than the abstracted merrymaking that goes on at a wake. The corpse was the Irish theatre, stricken down of an unknown disease in the prime of its life; and while the corpse was still lying in state the house caught fire and the wake had to be quickly transferred to a neighbour's home across the way.

Why do they not bury the corpse, everybody wants to know. Well, for two reasons. First a grand mausoleum is being designed and it would be a pity to waste the insurance money and the government grant by not building it. Then nobody is absolutely certain that the corpse might not sit up, like Dan Burke of *In the Shadow of the Glen*. It has twitched once or twice lately.

Outside the Abbey there was quite a spasm of liveliness only a year or so ago. It was caused by the arrival of a new play by Sean O'Casey at the Gaiety, where the ghosts of viceregal society still flit around in the foyers. *The Bishop's Bonfire* was being put on by Cyril Cusack, an Abbey-trained actor who has been seen in London but is also known in British and American film studios.

While the play was still in rehearsal, word was passed around that it was anti-Catholic and possibly even pro-Communist. A careful whispering campaign began, and there was immediate talk of rioting, stink-bombs, police cordons and all the trimmings which since the day of *The Playboy of the Western World* have been thought essential to the launching, in Dublin, of any play on a higher intellectual level than *Peg o' My Heart* or *Abie's Irish Rose*. English newspapermen flowed into the Shelbourne Hotel; Irish liquor flowed into English newspapermen and in no time at all the telephones were buzzing with stories of armoured cars ready to patrol the streets, police radio-cars cruising around the Gaiety, the Irish Air Force standing by with Spitfires, a document being drafted for submission to the Security Council. I can swear to it, at any rate, that I was told in the Shelbourne by a bright theatrical news-hawk from London that *The Bishop's Bonfire* would be stopped by the audience flinging rosary beads on to the stage if it could not be stopped any other way.

The nearest thing to a riot was among youngsters crowded on the footpath outside who booed and hissed and called for the manager. Their complaint was that they could not get into the gallery because it was full.

During the play there was a hiss every now and then and, towards the end, somebody did drop a stink-bomb which fell in the lap of a London producer's wife. He had been thinking that he might light up the West End with *The Bishop's Bonfire* but had changed his mind long before the stink-bomb was thrown.

All the elements were there for as great a night as the opening of *The Plough and the Stars*, but O'Casey himself did not come up to the occasion. Cusack is an old friend and had let me borrow the script of the play before rehearsals began. What I read led me to sit on the edge of my seat at the first night because I believed I was going to see O'Casey re-establish himself among his own countrymen, the only people who really understand him (and the only ones he understands). But it fell flat. A whole evening in the theatre cannot be a success just because O'Casey has put into his play some of the most comic of his writing; it cannot be a success because O'Casey has at last dropped the red poppycock which has spoiled so much of his non-theatrical writing in the last few years; it cannot succeed merely by being the best thing O'Casey has written for a long time. It could have been a triumph if the power of the best moments had been held. In spite of all the whipping up of anti-O'Casey feeling by the cheaper end of the Catholic Press, there was nothing the first-night audience wanted more than an unequivocal success.

Perhaps the *Bishop's Bonfire* production would hardly have been worth mentioning, except as showing how a live dramatist could revive the moribund Irish theatre. It is probably too late now for O'Casey to act Prince to Mr Blythe's Sleeping Beauty. I should not like this figure of speech to lead anyone into believing that I regard Mr Blythe as beautiful, or, for that matter, sleepy.

The Irish theatre can keep itself alive year after year on the work of writers like George Shiels, Lennox Robinson, Paul Vincent Carroll or Joseph Tomelty. But it needs an O'Casey at least once in twenty years if it is not to relapse into provincialism. There is no O'Casey in sight, and provincialism, at this moment, seems just around the corner.

The danger is made to seem even more imminent by the operations in Dublin of the Tennent management. During the war it became impossible for English touring companies to find travelling space for Irish visits. After the war the habit of importing plays seemed forgotten for a time, and the cost of transport seemed also to have become prohibitive. But in the last two or three years Dublin has once more appeared among the towns to be visited by English companies, and Tennents have even used it to try out plays on the way to London. The normal Dublin audience is more intelligent than the London first-night mob, and more likely to react to certain types of subtlety in dialogue. Whether it can guide an English manager who wants to finish off his production properly before bringing it to the West End is questionable, and I doubt if Tennents have learned much in that way up to now. But the presence of English plays with star names in them on the Dublin stage could develop into a serious thing for the Irish theatre. Dubliners are no less star-struck than Londoners, and their own theatres just now are very short indeed of stars, either real or synthetic.

I should distort the picture a little if I continued to write as though the Irish theatre consisted solely of the Abbey. The Gate Theatre, Dublin, is not to be overlooked though it is well past its peak.

Like the Abbey, the Gate was the creation of young men and women dissatisfied with the state of the Irish theatre. But the theatre the Gate protested against was the Abbey, and it was a very healthy thing for the Abbey to find in 1928 that its position was not unshakeable. The Gate youngsters were not committed to an all-Irish policy, and they began their first season with *Peer Gynt* on a stage fifteen feet wide in an auditorium holding 102 people.

Before long the Gate had its own theatre and was producing new Irish plays regularly, though they remained a minority of all its productions.

The Gate provided a more comfortable atmosphere for

Denis Johnston who, after having his first play, *The Moon in the Yellow River*, produced by the Abbey, had his second turned down. Other authors—not very productive ones on the whole—clustered round the Gate, but its most important contributions were in style of direction and of acting. Its stage décor made the Abbey, even though it still used some Gordon Craig settings, look almost Victorian; the acting at the Gate, being in a European rather than a purely Irish tradition, looked more alive.

Yet the Gate reached a climax and was on the road to decline all within a decade. There is a purely personal explanation for this, or for part of it. The Abbey companies had from the very first shown themselves most fissile and a whole chapter of Abbey history can be devoted to splits and quarrels, secessions, the formation of cliques and the persecution of enemies. The Gate proved to be subject to the same disease. Tensions and strains reached breaking point and the Gate had its inevitable splits. It is now weakened by the fact that management and tenancy of the theatre are divided between two groups each of which hold the stage for half the year. But there is still life in the old Gate. In the very week that *The Bishop's Bonfire* opened, the visiting critics from London were able to see a revival of Maura Laverty's *Liffey Lane* which had all the virtues of the more advanced Irish style. Miss Laverty does by theatrical *pointillisme* what O'Casey does, or used to, by broader strokes of poetic realism. She makes the sights and sounds and smells of the Dublin slums come alive, and jabs at their sores with a scalpel where O'Casey hacked with an axe.

In fifty years the Abbey and the Gate are virtually all that the Irish theatre has brought out of Ireland's bubbling genius for writing, acting and watching in the theatre. Some oddments in the Irish language have appeared, but the main influence of the language 'revival' has been to make the training of new young actors at the Abbey even more difficult. It is not merely a matter of finding somebody to teach them, but the management now insists on having a bilingual company. To say the least of it, this is unhelpful for a theatre which must always find, or at any rate always has found, its best plays written by Irishmen in the English language.

There are many reasons, then, why I say that it is questionable whether such a thing as 'the Irish theatre' now exists. Remnants exist. The Abbey itself exists, on however low a plane. A man like Cyril Cusack who gets hold of a play worth producing in Dublin can find the actors to fill the parts (though he has to borrow an Irishman from London to direct them). An audience like the one that crowded the Gaiety for the opening of *The Bishop's Bonfire* can be found in Dublin whenever a theatre offers some excitement.

But the actors, the audience, the writers are no longer fused as they were in the first ten years of the Abbey's life into a really national theatre. I still find, in London or New York, a lot of interest in what goes on in the Dublin theatres. I have seen a Boston audience lapping up a comedy by Paul Vincent Carroll (though Broadway took less kindly to it) and I feel sure we shall see that comedy in London. O'Casey still, in spite of being a Communist, earns most of his living from the United States; Denis Johnston lives by teaching English Literature to young women in New England, but none of this means that Irish authors are doing what they did for twenty years or so in this century—turning out a succession of plays of purely Irish inspiration which could cause equal excitement in other countries, especially England and the United States. In that sense I see no Irish theatre today, no successors to Yeats, Synge, O'Casey—or even to the more bread-and-butter writers like Lennox Robinson, St John Ervine or George Shiels. Paul Vincent Carroll seemed a hope for a time, but it has not come to much.

The reasons are easy to sense but not easy to define. Is it that English-speaking countries produce their best dramatists at times of national emotional excitement? The

Elizabethan-Jacobean time, the Restoration, the entry into the twentieth century show it in the English theatre. Until the Americans had the excitement of seeing their economy collapse they produced hardly any drama which was not copied from Europe—except Eugene O'Neill, who stopped writing anything that mattered at just about the same time as other Americans began to come up.

Ireland was excited between the 1890's and the 1920's by the abandonment of the Home Rule idea and the substitution of republicanism, by the fighting against the British and then between the two brands of republicans. While these excitements lasted there was a brilliant outburst of drama. But O'Casey, inspired by the violence of the 'twenties, was the last to produce original work successfully —and by original I mean not imitated consciously or otherwise from other dramatists.

Somebody else will have to be equally or comparably inspired before the three elements, actor, audience and writer are once more locked together in Ireland so that their work can again be seriously referred to as representing the Irish theatre.

Blood Wedding

Translated by Roy Campbell

To use the Cocteau definition, Frederico Garcia Lorca discovered in his three folk tragedies, Yerma, Blood Wedding *and* The House of Bernarda Alba *a poetry of the theatre. In these plays Lorca displays an intense poetic vision which increases in each play although the actual verse content is reduced, until in* The House of Bernarda Alba *we have the stark outlines of a tragedy, told with an economy and a force which follow the traditional art of the ballads. It was in his instinctive sense of the dramatic, a very Spanish sense as well, and his ability to communicate this to the audience through the untranslatable Spanish word 'duende' and so bring them into the performance (just as a Spanish audience is brought in to share the fortunes of a bull-fight or the tempo of a gipsy dance), that Lorca discovered his own poetry of the theatre. The following two passages from* Blood Wedding, *in Roy Campbell's translation, give us the two styles which alternate in this play: the first is a lyrical poem, the second pure drama pruned of all its trimmings. Whether Lorca's style is inimitably his own or whether others may follow him in this vein is hard to say, but there is no doubt that Lorca was not only a poet but also a poet of the theatre.*

(1) The Lullaby

MOTHER-IN-LAW [*sings*]:
>   Sing lullaby, baby,
>   About the great horse
>   Who wouldn't drink water,
>   So black was its course
>   Through the branches of Spring.
>   When it reaches the bridge
>   It lingers to sing.
>   Who can tell, baby,
>   What the water may bring

>Through its green halls
>With its long tail sweeping?

WIFE [*in a low voice*]:

>The horse will not drink
>Let your eyes close.

MOTHER-IN-LAW:

>The horse starts weeping
>Sleep, little rose.
>His mane is frozen,
>His hurt hoofs stagger,
>Between his eyes
>Is a silver dagger.
>They went to the water
>And there in the flood,
>Stronger than water
>The stream ran blood.

WIFE:

>The horse will not drink
>Let your eyes close.

MOTHER-IN-LAW:

>The horse starts weeping
>Sleep little rose.

WIFE:

>He would not taste it.
>Away from the bank
>With its silver flies
>His hot underlip shrank.
>To the hard mountains
>He whinnied remote
>With the dead river
>Over his throat.
>Ah! The great horse
>That dreaded the Flow!
>Horse of the daybreak!
>Grief of the snow!
>Wait! Do not come!

Shade the windows from beams
With dreams of branches
And branches of dreams.

MOTHER-IN-LAW:

My child is sleeping.

WIFE:

My child stops crying.

MOTHER-IN-LAW:

The horse, my baby,
On a pillow is lying.

WIFE:

Lullaby, baby.

MOTHER-IN-LAW:

Oh, the great horse,
That would not drink water.

WIFE:

Do not come! Do not enter!
To the mountain repair
Where in the grey valleys
You'll meet with the mare.

MOTHER-IN-LAW:

My child is sleeping.

WIFE:

My child is resting.

WIFE [*in a very soft voice*]:

The horse will not drink.
Let your eyes close.

MOTHER-IN-LAW [*rising, in a low voice*]:

The horse starts weeping.
Sleep, little rose.

> [*They take the child inside.*

(2) The Call to Action

Enter Leonardo's Wife

WIFE: They've fled. They've run away. She and Leonardo. On the horse. Locked in each other's arms, they went off like a shooting star!

FATHER: It's not true! My daughter! No!

MOTHER: Your daughter! Yes! The sprout of a wicked mother! And he, himself, as well. But now she's the wife of my son!

BRIDEGROOM [*entering*]: Let's follow! Who has a horse?

MOTHER: Who has a horse, now, this moment? Who's got a horse? I'll give all that I have, to my eyes and my tongue. . . .

VOICE: Here's one!

MOTHER: Go on! After them! [*He goes out, with* TWO YOUTHS.] No. Don't go. Those people kill quickly and well . . . but yet, gallop, and I'll come behind.

FATHER: It can't be she. Perhaps she's thrown herself into the cistern.

MOTHER: The pure and honourable throw themselves into the water. Not that one, no! But now, she's the wife of my son! Two clans. Here there are two clans. [*Everybody comes in.*] My family and yours. Clear out of here, everyone; shake the dust off your shoes. We'll go and help my son. [*The people separate into two groups.*] Because there are plenty of people. His cousins from the sea, and all those from inland. Come on out of here! Down all the roads! The hour of blood has come once more! Two clans—you with yours, and I with mine! Get back! Get back!

CURTAIN

The Scottish Scene

*

by Charles Graves

AT THE ENTRANCE to the Outlook Tower, that remarkable Edinburgh centre which was his creation, Sir Patrick Geddes caused to be placed a diagrammatic embodiment of his conception of society. In the main it read something like this:—'City—Nation—Europe—The World!' Geddes was the apostle of regionalism, which has entered so strongly into the structure of the British Broadcasting Corporation, and, though his creed attracted few adherents while he lived, being a little too nebulous for most people, probably nothing has been quite the same in Scotland since his time. The young Scottish nationalist of today hardly realizes that in Geddes he had a progenitor whose creed, like his own, entered into every aspect of his existence.

It is the growth of this philosophy which makes it useless to seek in a general way an answer to the question of how the theatre in Scotland is faring, for the theatre in Scotland is only half the story. Side by side with it, and sometimes overlapping it, there is the Scottish theatre. So long as James Bridie lived the overlap was considerable, and though there is a tendency for youth to feel that Barrie's sentimentality cancels his virtues as a dramatic craftsman, we cannot say that the overlap has ceased to exist while plays like *Mary Rose* and *Dear Brutus* are revived.

The majority of contemporary Scottish playwrights, however, look for Scottish themes in a way that neither Barrie nor Bridie did. It would be idle to deny that many of them would welcome a London success, but I do not think that they have this first and foremost in their minds. In the majority of cases the type of play they write precludes it.

That it is possible, however, for a thoroughly Scottish play to succeed outside Scotland was proved long ago by the success of Graham Moffat's *Bunty Pulls the Strings*, and more recently by the triumph of *The Dashing White Sergeant*. This comedy was first acted in Dundee in April 1954, and since then it has been seen on innumerable stages from Orkney to Hammersmith. It is a typical repertory play, as we know repertory today, and the character of the fifteen-year-old girl, spoiled for schooling in this country by a taste of American life at an impressionable age, is not exclusively Scottish in its appeal nor does it inevitably ask for a Scottish interpreter. Indeed, the part was created with great vivacity by a young Cornish actress of much promise, Hazel Penwarden.

The rewards of dramatists writing for the Scottish stage are modest indeed and would be still more modest but for the windfalls of radio and television. It must be remembered, however, that a little over thirty years ago they simply did not exist. It was not until 1921, when the Scottish National Players announced their first production, that the Scottish playwright found a sure field for the purely Scottish play. Between 1921 and 1940 the company produced 130 plays, and over half of them were new. Among its producers was Tyrone Guthrie and among its actresses the late Elliot Mason.

The Scottish National Players disappeared officially and finally in 1950, and when they quitted the Scottish theatrical scene the picture had greatly changed. For by that time four repertory companies were in existence in Scotland. The one which came nearest to carrying on the work upon which the Scottish National Players had been engaged—the furthering of Scottish drama—was the Glasgow Citizens' Theatre, and this was not surprising, seeing that the guiding hand in this venture, until his death in January 1951, was

James Bridie, who, as 'Mary Henderson', had written for the National Players.

The other three repertory companies stood in a different relation to the aspirations which inspired the Citizens'. Two of them—those of Perth and Dundee—had their origins outside Scotland, and though both of them have staged Scottish premières, they cannot be said to be deliberately national in their policy. Nor, in the first place, could the Edinburgh Gateway Theatre—in its inception a remarkable venture, since it was the only theatre in the world sponsored by a Church. But, though the Gateway Theatre was nominally run by the Church of Scotland through its Home Board, its conduct was delegated to a Director with wide discretionary powers in the choice of play to be staged. The theatre underwent several phases of existence, the plays at one time being presented by amateurs, at another by a resident professional company. The responsibility for them is no longer that of the Church, the theatre having been leased to a company controlled by Scottish directors whose greatest successes have been achieved with new Scottish plays.

While there exists, both in Glasgow and Edinburgh, considerable support for a Scottish theatre, it cannot be claimed that, in these days of heavy production costs and uncertain audiences, its future is assured. The Glasgow Citizens' Theatre has had its own problems to face, not the least of which was the expiry of its lease of the Princess's Theatre in the Gorbals, which has been its home for the last ten years. A satisfactory arrangement was arrived at, under which Glasgow Corporation agreed to buy the theatre and rent it to the company at £1,250 a year, plus rates. This should ensure the continuance of the work there, but, though the Gorbals is easily accessible from other parts of Glasgow, its situation on the South Bank of the Clyde is not attractive to some sections of the community.

Scotland has had a long theatrical history which goes back to medieval times and to the performances of the old Robin

Hood plays, for their right to stage which the Edinburgh populace contended fiercely. It is a history which is less broken than is generally supposed, though for some periods the records are tenuous. They do not abound in the names of great plays, and, if the greatness of the theme which gave rise to David Lindsay's *Satire of the Three Estates* is not to be denied, there is general consent that the overwhelming success of this play on the stage of the Edinburgh International Festival, both when it was first acted there in 1948 and when it was revived in 1951, was due in large measure to the skill and showmanship of Tyrone Guthrie. The search for native worth which the triumph of *The Three Estates* prompted revealed little else of comparable merit, and the Scottish stage has ceased to think in terms of revivals and is now devoting itself to the production of modern plays, in the hope that it may eventually produce a masterpiece or two.

To this end many native playwrights are engaged. Robert McLellan's imagination inclines to the historic, or at any rate to the costume play, yet his work shows an impressive use of Scots and of the stage. Robert Kemp, most prolific of contemporary Scottish dramatists, has done nothing better than his adaptations of *The Three Estates* and Molière's *L'Ecole des Femmes*, unless it is his play on Burns in Edinburgh, *The Other Dear Charmer*. R. J. B. Sellar is rapidly shaping as a popular writer of comedy, but scored a distinct success with his *Brief Glory*, an historical play on the fortunes of Prince Charles Edward. Moray McLaren's play on Stevenson's Edinburgh, *Heather on Fire*, has shape, colour and emotional content. A. D. Mackie has boldly assayed contemporary themes, yet his best contribution so far is a one-act play on the wartime anti-Italian riots in Edinburgh. Alexander Reid has been most successful in the dovetailing of two legendary themes in *The Lass wi' the Muckle Mou'*, and in *The Warld's Wonder* showed that he could blend poetry with comedy in a fashion suited to the stage. Ian Dallas, in *The Face of Love*, is nearer to

G

the modern poetic drama of England and France than to
the native school.

Perhaps the dead hand of ecclesiastical authority which
lay heavily on the Scottish stage in the past has proved too
much for an easy *risorgimento*, and there are parts of Scotland
in which the hostility to the stage engendered by the Church
is even now no dead letter. In the great centres of popula-
tion, however, no animus against the theatre remains, but
there, as elsewhere, it seems certain that the persecution of
the past has bred a sad lack of critical appreciation on the
part of present-day audiences. The provincial manner in
which plays containing the most trite and conventional
jokes are received with acclaim, though they have little
dramatic merit either in construction or writing, is a danger
which faces the attempt to create a Scottish theatre.

This lack of critical discrimination is, of course, not
entirely, or perhaps mainly, traceable to sources in the past.
It is due in great measure to economic factors which have
resulted in a change in the constitution of theatre audiences.
In recent years the professional classes as a whole have
tended more and more to abandon the theatre, whose patrons
are now drawn chiefly from the bourgeois or shopkeeping
classes. This alone has led to a corresponding change in the
type of play which is popular. The sables and shirt-fronts
which graced the boxes and the stalls thirty-five years
ago enjoyed the intellectual dialogue of Shaw, the social
comedy of Galsworthy, the invention of Lonsdale and the
fantasy of Barrie. Today these things are largely or wholly
out of favour. What attracts is comedy of the family type,
the 'whodunit' and the American musical, though the Savoy
operas, while not quite the social occasion they once were,
are still hugely popular.

Improvement in transport, with the facilities offered by
the railways and bus companies, have, as elsewhere, put
the city theatres of Scotland within reach of the country
patron, now perhaps whetted for dramatic pleasures through
his taste of community drama, or stirred to appreciate the

theatre by the touring companies sent out from Perth and Dundee or the Gateway Theatre. There have been stirrings, too, in places like St Andrews, Ayr, Dumfries, Annan and Greenock.

In the big cities this means little more than that blocks of seats are booked by the country visitors for the latest 'musicals', some of which, in places like Glasgow, run for perhaps nine weeks. Nor are the annual summer shows and the pantomimes less popular with the same clientele. In many cases the runs of these have for some years been fantastic.

Theatre, as we knew it thirty years ago, seems dead in the great cities of Scotland—for the major part of the year at least. It is only for periods in the spring and autumn that it flourishes, and the pity is that when a play of considerable dramatic merit, such as Anouilh's *The Lark*, comes our way, almost (as it sometimes seems) by accident, the response is far short of what it should be. It is then that one really despairs of the future. I am not blaming theatre managements for this state of affairs. If they did not pay their way (and their shareholders) there would be no theatres. On the contrary, I rejoice that our lot in Scotland is not worse than it is.

The dominion exercised by the modern audience has also had an ill effect upon repertory. Either that, or managements are timid in the extreme. That the former is the case seems borne out by the evidence to be found in Wilson Barrett's *On Stage for Notes*, in which he lists the losses on his Shakespearian productions in Edinburgh. It is only fair to say that his experience with the same plays in Glasgow has been different. If further proof were needed, it might be found in the financial loss which resulted during the short season given by some members of the Wilson Barrett Company at the Gateway Theatre, which included fine performances of *The Three Sisters* and *Winterset*, or in the enterprising directorship of Herbert Wise at Dundee Repertory Theatre, which was far too enterprising to last.

Here Mr Wise, greatly daring, mounted performances of such plays as Henry de Montherlant's *La Reine Morte* and Humbert Wolfe's *The Silent Knight*.

After Mr Wise's departure for the south came the sad decision of Mr Wilson Barrett to strike camp and disperse. His seasons in Edinburgh, Glasgow and Aberdeen had for long been a feature of the social life of those cities. While Mr Barrett produced few new plays and ventured few unusual revivals, he kept a steady level of production, introducing Scotland to West End successes which had not reached it on tour. Moreover, his audiences could always rely upon the way in which he mounted his plays. His absence has been greatly missed, but his resolve to disband his company was founded upon a feeling that the distraction of TV was likely to affect his audiences adversely for too long for him to be able to stand the pace. There are today signs that this view was perhaps not altogether justified.

In Perth the management has been singularly skilful in its choice of play and also, perhaps, singularly fortunate in its audience, since it has been able to stage not only the classics of drama, including Shakespeare, but plays by modern French and English writers as well as a fair proportion of English plays. In recent years, by creating a second company, it has also been able to tap that rapidly growing centre of civic life, Kirkcaldy, where it would like to see a theatre built which could adequately house its productions.

Despite the challenge of television which here, as elsewhere, is no doubt making itself felt to the disadvantage of the living stage, the theatre in Scotland is by no means dead. At any rate none of the leading commercial houses has been threatened by closure or forced to prolong its existence by recourse to films or variety.

Notes from Norway

*

by Olav Paus Grunt

THE WORD *crisis* has a way of turning up every now and then in connexion with the theatre in Norway, as elsewhere. More than any of the other art forms the theatre lies exposed to the fluctuations of economic conditions, or at the mercy of sudden and fickle changes of taste. There are crises all the time, and the latest one is upon us as I write this. Norway is not the only country where the decline in audience attendance is causing concern and is becoming symptomatic with the dangerously low ebb of worth-while new plays. But if no one can say that the Norwegian drama is today exactly flourishing, certainly no one can deny that the theatre is held by us—as it is in the other Scandinavian countries—in high esteem.

For a country of only three million people the range of our theatrical activities remains considerable. Oslo itself, which even including its suburbs has less than half a million inhabitants, is able to support five straight theatres and two music halls. The fact that four of these five theatres receive subsidies (three considerable amounts, the other a very small grant) will be of interest to theatre lovers in cities where theatres do not receive such 'official' encouragement. Our oldest and most respected theatre if you like, is the National Theatre (*Nationalteateret*), but there also exists a second national theatre, of more recent origin and more limited appeal, *Det Norske Teater* (The Norwegian Theatre), to meet the demands of Norway's second official language 'landsmål'. (Perhaps a comment on this anomalous situation is necessary. 'Landsmål' was originally an artificially created amalgam of spoken dialects, presenting certain analogies with 'Provençal', the main difference being that 'landsmål' has a wider and more profound historical and social significance, and through its official status has acquired a position whereby it is understood by everybody, but yet remains far less spoken and written than the other Norwegian language 'bokmål', the language of Ibsen and of the vast majority of townspeople, whatever their social background.) The third major Oslo theatre to receive subsidies has been in operation for nearly three years, the *Folketeater* (The People's Theatre), which is housed in an enormous building, a creation of the social-minded 'thirties, and lies near Oslo's East End in an effort to bring the theatre to the working classes.

Theatres which wish to obtain public funds can only qualify through programmes of undoubted literary quality, and it is always the educational value of good theatre which is stressed. The tradition has grown to take the theatre seriously. Thus we see that even *Det Nye Teater* (The New Theatre), which in spite of a very small grant from the municipality of Oslo depends on the box-office for its continued existence, aims at offering artistic performances and pays frequent tribute, in between lighter works, to serious drama. Only one theatre in Oslo, the *Centralteateret*, devotes itself wholly to the task of providing sheer fun. And it is a little sadly that I have to admit that it is the only one to be financially quite sound, at any rate so far.

There are regularly subsidized theatres in Bergen, Trondheim and Stavanger. But it is the state-operated *Riksteater*, run exclusively as a permanent touring company, which is the most interesting experiment and indeed innovation. The *Riksteater* gave its first performance in July 1949 at Kirkenes, close to the Russian frontier. The choice was deliberate, a token of the desire to bring first rate theatrical productions even to the most remote localities. Once again the State has come to the rescue to ensure that good theatre should be taken seriously and available for all.

State subsidies are also granted to *Teaterskolen*, a dramatic school recently founded, whose students are recruited from the whole country. For quite some time individual theatres have had their theatre schools, training their young hopefuls, but this inevitably proved a strain on their economy. Consequently their efforts were fused, and the result was the creation of the new theatre school. The subjects taught include the history of world drama, analysis of plot and character in plays, voice production and diction, thorough study of our two official languages, study of foreign languages, especially English, physical training, fencing, ballet, etc. Efforts have also been made to introduce pupils of secondary schools to the living theatre through the *Skoleteater* (School theatre), which arranges a certain number of productions at special matinée performances for them, where the prices are very moderate, or provides a certain number of seats at ordinary performances, also at moderate prices.

So much for the framework within which the theatre in Norway operates. With the support the actor gains a fair measure of economic security, and the theatre can afford opportunities for serious dramatic literature hardly shared by the purely commercial theatre of, say, Broadway. Plays are not always produced with an eye to the box office, quite the contrary; classical plays, both foreign and Norwegian, as well as the more difficult experimental work of contemporary writers, have been brought to our theatre-goers. The last few months, which have in no way been exceptional, have enabled us to see at Oslo two Shakespeare productions (*Macbeth* and *Othello*), plays by Ibsen and Bjørnson, a couple of new Norwegian plays, Tchekhov's *Three Sisters*, Brecht's *Mutter Courage*, Anouilh's *L'Alouette*, Pirandello's *Liolà*, Lorca's *Yerma*, Beckett's *En attendant Godot*, Fry's *Phoenix too frequent* and *The Dark is Light Enough* and Rice's *Street Scene*. Whatever else our theatre may be, we can claim to be more consistently cosmopolitan than London, Paris, or New York, and this may be said to be true of all

the Scandinavian capitals, where conditions similar to
those in Oslo prevail.

If, however, we examine the artistic achievements instead
of the social climate of our theatre, the picture is less rosy.
For some reason the theatre does not seem to have completely recovered from the disruptive effects of the German
occupation. There exists today a widespread dissatisfaction
with our present state of acting and directing, though this
is largely due, it must in fairness be explained, to the vivid
memories of what has become the 'golden age' of the
Norwegian theatre. The warm afterglow could still be felt
in the 'twenties and even well into the 'thirties. After all,
Scandinavia had at the turn of the century been the sensa-
tional centre of some of the best dramatists in the world,
with Ibsen, Bjørnson and Strindberg. Out of this climate
of enthusiasm we enjoyed a great theatrical art.

Not so today! It must have been a shock to many
Norwegians when that fine English actress Peggy Ashcroft
and a company of English actors came across recently
and showed us a better production of *Hedda Gabler* than we
had seen for a very very long time. It would hardly be fair
to expect all Norwegian Ibsen productions to reach such a
quality which must be rare even in London's West End,
and I should be loath to give the impression that the
Norwegian theatre is backward or provincial. It is not!
We follow pretty closely whatever impulses come from
Broadway's best directors, from Barrault and Vilar in Paris,
from London or Stratford. What we generally lack are the
qualities of consummate skill and precise artistry which we
occasionally see on our travels or with visiting companies.
Alas, even our best productions are seldom free of such
blemishes as slowness of rhythm, inadequate diction, and
a certain gaucheness of mannerism. But having to put on
new productions fairly frequently is not conducive to the
exquisite finish which counts for so much, and the somewhat
limited range of artists for casting purposes, to say nothing
of a real need for first-class directors, means that there is

a desperate struggle in the maintenance of decent standards. We have competence, but seldom great inspiration.

And the public? I started these notes by stating that the audiences have shown a tendency to turn their backs on the theatre. Time and time again we have witnessed great dramatists, in productions well above average, failing to find a public in spite of an enthusiastic Press. Sometimes even Ibsen fails, and the fashionable contemporaries such as Anouilh or Tennessee Williams cannot always be relied upon to find an audience.

Nobody knows how things will develop in the Norwegian theatre over the next few years. The public, so often unfaithful, is nevertheless instinctively drawn towards the theatre and is willing to pay for the values it can offer. When an outstanding performance comes along (such as Peggy Ashcroft's 'Hedda') enthusiasm knows no limits. We have laid our hopes and faith in the future by starting an officially run dramatic school. The *Riksteater* tours will rouse interest in the drama among people who had never seen a play before. Somehow one does not have to be incurably an optimist to believe that the theatre will survive.

Partage de Midi

A scene from the play by Paul Claudel
translated by Lothian Small

YSÉ: Do not leave me, Mesa!
        Oh God!
        Can I possibly be saved? I see it now! I see it all!
        How terrible the things that I have done!

MESA: What do you see?

YSÉ: A hovel made of reeds, a dead man
        With a terrifying look, under an enormous tuft of
           black hair!
        Racked by cholera, a nauseating blanket thrown over
           him.
        But it was not that stale air that I was loathing!
        And all the time water dropping from the roof
        Right on the eyeball staring from the socket.
        And outside rain as I never saw it rain before, a
           deluge, a forest gloomy as arum leaves,
        And every shaft of rain a pipe-stem thick.

MESA: What else do you see?

YSÉ: Suffering, poignant pain!

MESA: What else?

YSÉ: Oh my children!
        What a poor mother I was for you! I see them. How
           intently
        They would watch with their calm, trusting eyes
        While I—they loved their mother—was reading
           aloud
        And to think I have deceived, abandoned, murdered
           them!
        And waking sometimes in the night I heard while
           they slept their separate breathing

I listened with beating heart and knew they were
    my dear children!
They never were lovelier, you know. They never
    caused me sorrow.
Everybody's eyes were on us when we went out,
I the young mother triumphant beside my sons, with
    one walking each side of me
Head erect, fists clenched, little soldiers marching.
I do not understand. I am only a poor unfortunate
    woman. How did it all come about?

MESA: It is *love* that did everything. But is love then no
    longer for us the one thing good and true, just
    and charged with meaning?
Have even words lost their sense? And do we no
    longer call
The *good* whatever fosters
Our love, and *evil* its adversary?
Do they not call it 'the triumph of nature and life'?
Death severed the links no more surely.
Did not so just and pure a union as ours deserve
    greatly? So very pure.
We certainly never greatly spared
The others, but did we ever greatly spare ourselves?
We are come to this. I, my limbs bruised, like a
    malefactor on the while,
And you, with outraged soul, leaving the body
    behind, like a sword half unsheathed!

YSÉ: Why such dreadful words? Do be quiet.

MESA: The best alone is the best, Ysé.
That is the great imperishable Commandment. But
    evil itself
Bears its own good with it and we must not let it
    perish. Calling the dead back to life
Is beyond our power, but our own death still is ours.
So we can in all fairness turn to the Avenger
And say: 'We are come. From what is ours take
    your due.' So much can we do.

And
Since you now are free
And there still abides within us ready to be destroyed
   the indestructible power
Of all the sacraments become a greater one through
   the mystery of mutual consent
Your body is my body, Ysé. See, God, this my
   body!
Your body is my body, and in that sole pledge
Is the avowal, and in penitence accepted
The law, and in supreme confirmation
The founding of our Order for evermore.

YSÉ: Your body is my body, Mesa.
MESA: All is consummated, my soul.
YSÉ: Then have no fear.
MESA: I have no fear, Ysé.
YSÉ: Even in the old days, dear child-like Mesa
       You could not hide from me what you were thinking,
          your eyes told everything.
       But now
       As naturally as we smell with the nose and touch
          with our fingertips,
       That is how (it is almost laughable how guileless
          and good, how wholehearted and healthy, how
          incomparable),
       Yes, that is how I see you, Mesa,
       See your soul by my very own
       Even each thought it conceives
       And by my own life's rhythms feel how you live and
          move and have your being.
MESA: Can you also see my fear in the face of death?
YSÉ: Don't be ashamed of it, dear Mesa. It is the being
          most alive who most dreads
       To be no more! Oh how hard and closed in men
          are, how afraid to come out and suffer and
          die!
       But woman the female, mother of man,

Is not astonished—she is too familiar with the silent
    hands that pull.
It is I, you see, who am now consoling and comfort-
    ing you.

MESA: You are still sleeping while I am awake.

YSÉ: It is come full circle.
I see your heart, Mesa, I am content.
And now the whole past with the good and all the
    evil
And the penitence binding the two are no more than
    a foundation and a beginning making a single
    whole
With what is, what at present exists for evermore.
I was jealous, Mesa, and I saw you gloomy, and I
    knew
You were concealing from me something of your-
    self.
But now I see the whole, and I am wholly seen and
    there is nothing in us but love,
Naked, pure, finding life each in the other, in
    interpenetration
Ineffable, in the voluptuous joy of wedded difference,
    man and woman become two great spiritual
    animals,
Life of all this mutual throbbing within us of the
    seeing spirit,
Heart of this heart under the heart in us whence
    come flesh and spirit and hair and embracing arms
And vision and sense, and the lips so long since one
    with yours.
—Oh do not laugh at me, Mesa!

MESA: I am feeling the hidden deep down in you.

YSÉ: Oh Mesa, if you knew how awful it is for a woman,
    To see herself in the mirror, see age creeping on and
      those tell-tale lines on her face
    To sense at a touch one is oneself no more, to feel
      the once maiden body,

Fresh and iris-bright grown heavy and hard a
    stone!

Oh the fiancée her lips like white hyacinth on fresh
    moss

But I shall grow old no more! Now I am young for
    ever!

MESA: Now it is you teaching me while I listen. How long
    will it be, woman fruit of the vine,

    Before I drink you anew in the city of God?

YSÉ: That I neither see nor understand, Mesa. But as
    each creates

    His vision and understanding, so it is with his own
    life

    He finds his source of wonder in the one thing which
    is

    His own span of life. It is no use trying to under-
    stand me.

MESA: Then what do you see? What do you understand?

YSÉ: Only your heart.

MESA: What else?

YSÉ: You must not be afraid! Our own time throbbing
    on, the old time running down,

    The device at the top of the house, with only a few
    minutes left, just the time

    For the explosion, scattering to the winds this bodily
    temple. Do not be afraid.

MESA: Though the base flesh flinch the spirit remains stead-
    fast.

    Like the solitary candle watching in the night

    Layer upon layer of the dark will not suffice

    To quench the feeble flame!

    Take heart, my soul! Of what avail was I here
    below?

    I never knew.

    You and I cannot, Ysé, give ourselves by halves!
    Let us then give ourselves wholly now!

    Already I feel within me

All the old powers of my being setting out for a
  new order.

I am hearing beyond the tomb the Destroyer's
  heralds forming up,

The summons to the judgment seat's fathomless
  solitude,

And here, to the sounds of imperishable bronze,

All that was my life mustered before my eyes

Fraying out like notes from some ageing trumpet.

[YSÉ, *with her eyes closed and her arms crossed, rises and
  stands up before* MESA. *A strong gust of wind lifts her
  hair.*

YSÉ: Look at me now, Mesa, while there still is
  time.

Look at me here upright stretching out like a great
  olive tree in the earth's moon-beams, the light of
  its night.

Bear in mind the look on this mortal face for the
  moment of our decision is at hand and you will
  see me no more with the eyes of the flesh!

I hear you without hearing you, for already I have
  mortal ears no more! Do not be silent, beloved,
  you are there.

And only give me the note, that . . .

Arise and hear my own golden tones

Beginning, swelling out like pure song and like a
  voice attuned to yours, better than all instruments,
  your Ysé for ever.

Under you I have been the flesh that yields, like
  a horse between your knees, the animal not
  impelled by reason,

Like a horse making for wherever you veer its head,
  like a horse carried faster and farther than you
  desire!

Look upon her now, Mesa, wholly unfolded, the
  woman incarnating a beauty deployed in the
  greater beauty!

Why wait for a shrill trumpet? Arise, oh shattered
  form, and look on me as a listening dancer.
Her little jubilant feet gathered into the irresistible
  rhythm.
Follow me, delay no more!
Great God, I am come, laughing, swaying, released
  from all roots, leaning back on the very essence
  of light as on the wing poised above the waves!
Oh Mesa, here is night with its great rift! and here
  am I ready to go free,
The sign for the last time of this great profusion of
  hair all wild in the wind of death.

MESA: Adieu! I have looked on you for the last time!
By what long painful paths
Far off still yet bearing ever
One upon the other are we going
To lead our souls in travail?
Remember, yes, remember the sign!
Mine is not hair tossing idly in the storm or a hand-
  kerchief waving for a moment,
No, it is myself, all veils flung aside, the powerful
  searing flame, the great male in the glory of God,
Man in his August splendour, the Spirit triumphant
  in transfiguration at the zenith.

Encouraging the young playwright.   The Bristol Old Vic's production of *Marching Song*, by John Whiting.

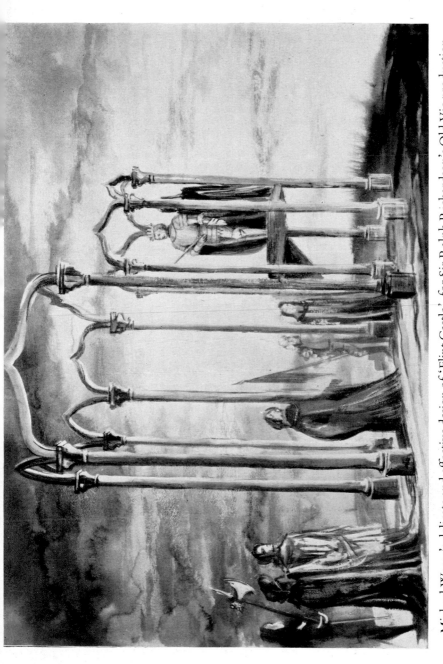

Michael Warre's delicate and effective design of 'Flint Castle', for Sir Ralph Richardson's Old Vic production of *Richard II*.

Tanya Moiseiwitsch's décor for Tyrone Guthrie's Stratford production of *Henry VIII*, one of the best examples of modern Shakespeare.

Those Who Can't, Criticize

*

by Iain Hamilton

DRAMATIC CRITICS come in many varieties, each with his own pocketful of manias, each almost visibly enhaloed with his own swarm of bees and bats, and well might one despair of finding categories to cram them into. Having been at the curious business for a decade myself (this is for me a sort of celebration in which the gentle reader may join if he enjoys a lowish and desultory sort of party), I find it a truly formidable task to abstract from my long and close observations of, on the one hand, Willy the one and only, the prime exhibitionist of the tribe, and, on the other, Aloysius, who sits so meekly and thankfully with the text on his knee and the gleam of devotion in his eye that one might imagine he had actually paid for his seat, and all the ragtag and bobtail in between—I find it, I say, a laborious business to abstract a little order from the Babelish chaos which is reflected daily and weekly for your guidance and amusement.

*   *   *

But first we had better be clear as to the precise nature of the subject. By dramatic critic I mean simply someone who occupies a free seat in a theatre and who, for modest gain, publishes in a daily or weekly newspaper or magazine his reactions to each particular experience. That is to say, I mean a journalizing reviewer who may or may not be gifted with some critical aptitude, and not a dramatic critic

at all if you are so high-minded as to take the phrase to
denote a practitioner of that high branch of literary criticism
which by virtue of subject is prefixed dramatic. Some talk
of Aristotle and some of Eliot, of Dryden and of Coleridge
and such great names as these. But not, for the moment, I.
Gosson is our ancestor, Clement Scott our plaster saint.
We are all tainted with unoriginal sins.

Yet the party is to be kept moderately clean: we must,
however regretfully, exclude such provincial apprentices
as have the task—laid down by their editors, as laid down
to them by the advertising managers—of uttering bromides
designed to soothe the theatre managers and that large
and squashy section of the public which seeks only 'entertainment' (and 'entertainment', as you know, permits of no
qualitative considerations). Criticism in the sense of just
description and keen analysis, leading it may well be to
more or less adverse judgement, is bad form in a great
many corners of this liberty-loving and logic-loathing
island, and strenuously discouraged on the dimmer margins
of our free press.

At an early stage in my own career (if I may be so im-
modest as to strike a personal note—in the best tradition
of play-reviewing—so early in the proceedings) I was
taken aside by a certain Editor-in-Chief who found my
reviewing a shade too caustic, and instructed by him that
if I really wanted to learn how to review satisfactorily in
terms appropriate to and suitable for the newspaper concerned I had better bloody well take away this here volume
of press cuttings (his own, by God) and study it carefully.
I did so, and what I discovered were the hand-outs of
press agents sub-edited sufficiently to allow the intrusion of
the first personal pronoun at regular intervals. He gave
his advice seriously, with no suspicion of irony. 'Look
where I am now,' his attitude proclaimed. But this was
really too simple, even for me. Besides, at that point in
time I had no wish to be an Editor-in-Chief. So, priggishly,
I handed back the volume of cuttings and got myself

another job where, within the limits of obscure laws and of good taste reasonably interpreted, a man might think his thoughts and express them as he saw fit and have them print in one piece.

So much for our rat-race in its lower reaches.

*   *   *

Now, dramatic critics may in the first instance be divided into whole-time specialists, the minority (the boys who have their desks surrounded by dictionaries of quotations and filing-cabinets containing the works of other dramatic critics, and who have reference books which will tell you exactly how many hours Madame Bienpuante spent in the service of the Comédie Française in 1862), and part-timers (the majority) like myself. I don't know that I need make any further distinction between them except to repeat gravely that in the nature of things the whole-timers tend to be better up in gossip about the darlings of the painted stage and for that reason are in greater peril of becoming altogether too esoterically partisan. As for the part-timers, we are poor things but, on the whole, above suspicion.

Whole-time or part-time, there are two rather more arbitrary distinctions which can profitably be made to help you arrive at some sort of understanding of the animal. Your dramatic critic will tend to take either himself more seriously than his subject or his subject more seriously than himself; he is all too seldom able to strike a balance between, on the one hand, his desire to shine and scintillate, and, on the other, whatever suspicion lingers that his duty is not merely to be himself another entertainer. Secondly, your dramatic critic will tend to attach the greater degree of importance either to the play itself (in which case he had better have some sort of literary sense) or to the players (and here the descriptive talent is useful). In order to bring these two sets of distinctions together into one, we may say, that roughly speaking, your exhibitionist, for whom dramatic criticism is nothing more than a means to a personal end (notoriety, bank balance, and power over the darlings), will probably concentrate on players and performance; and that your more seriously, literary-critically, minded reviewer will in all likelihood place his emphasis on the play itself and be somewhat perfunctory about the performers and producer. In theory, I suppose, there is no reason why a paragon fully equipped with all the virtues should not suddenly appear in the arena, putting us all, the scintillating Willies with their verbal penny-crackers and the sombre Aloysiuses with their dismal qualifications, to shame; but I must count it extremely unlikely in practice, for such a hero would almost certainly be able to find more agreeable and profitable employment elsewhere. In writing plays, for example. Those who can, said Shaw, do; and those who can't, criticize.

E sempre così! (This is one of our characteristics, the giving of tone to a notice by the odd foreign phrase. *Voilà tout!* Look! No hands!)

Except, of course, in the upper air where you find such as Shaw himself using dramatic criticism as a mere bull-dozing device to clear the obstacles that clutter up his own road to success as a dramatist.

*   *   *

But let us for diversion digress; let us consider the general truth of Shaw's witticism, so often frenziedly denied by critics who are quite certain they could write a masterpiece if only they had time, and by playwrights who are sure they know a good play when they see one but spend an unconscionable time in the carpentry of bad ones. The practice of more or less detached criticism (even if there is only the merest modicum of literary criticism informing it) has a stiffening, if not totally inhibiting, effect upon the creative-imaginative faculty, and it is a lamentable fact that even the wisest and most imaginative of critics is only too likely, should he stray across the border, to produce the most formless, banal, and facetious play—and to be distressed when other critics point this out, at worst with open and gleeful malice, at best by damning with the feeblest of faint praise.

An admirable critic of my acquaintance—but no; on second thoughts it would be embarrassing. . . .

If we may for a little descend, not actually *to*, I trust, but—shall we say?—*towards* the ridiculous, perhaps you will allow me to cite my own sad case.

After a few years of more or less respectable dramatic criticism in dailies and weeklies I had the misfortune to be visited with the idea for a play, and the further misfortune to write that play, and the ultimate calamity to have the play accepted for production by an arts theatre. It was directed by a producer who happened to be a good one and performed by a company who did me the honour of liking the poor thing. It was chosen to reopen a reconstructed theatre in the presence of sundry dignitaries, civic and otherwise. And it ran (or at any rate staggered forward) for a fortnight. I was in Italy at the time of the production, arriving home in time to see the final performance, and later, by this time in a suicidal state of mind, to open the envelope of press cuttings which had kindly been assembled against my return.

As to the thoughts that boiled in my brain as I sat at the back of the dress circle and watched the game efforts of the players to breathe their own warm life into my straight-jacketed text, decency requires me to keep them to myself. But I am willing, as a dramatic critic, to disclose to you the fact that other dramatic critics were not wholly enamoured of the play which some of them had travelled a fair distance to see. And I do this not out of any agreeable masochism but rather because, now that merciful time has healed the wounds, I see that the experience was of some value to me and might conceivably be of some enlightenment to other young bravos contemplating a similar step.

If one is not a critic but a creator, wholly abandoned to the painful pleasure that is work for him, one may properly say, 'To hell with the critics!' and know that one's peers will, more or less, making all allowances for natural malice and envy, provide the necessary support and comfort. But if one is a critic, and by nature a fairly severe and priggish one, and if one's incursion into dramaturgy is damned by one's peers, whence is comfort to be drawn?

It was not drawn by me, I can assure you, from the words of praise and encouragement with which my critics interlarded their serious objections to the enterprise. So I shall invite you to take these as read and to consider instead the barbéd darts which burst the balloon.

'The play,' said the *Manchester Guardian*, 'is obviously the work of a new dramatist not altogether sure of his hand. Some of his characterization is shadowy, and at times the dialogue tends to relapse into a kind of stilted formalism. The play's most serious fault is, however, the totally unconvincing decision, etc., etc.'

Alas, how many such sentences had I myself set down in the heat of battle!

'The cast', said the *Scotsman*, in accents still more severe, 'played it for what it was worth. But just what that worth was proved to be rather a variable quantity in dramatic algebra. For the piece wavers uncertainly between reality and fantasy ... there is too much talking *in vacuo*, and rather specious political talking at that. It is as if the Scottish kailyard was in the doldrums, despite some gilded barbs from Sartre and Marx to liven it. The air was too humourless. ...'

Ah me! And Mr Randolph Churchill is forever writing articles about the Press, complaining that dog don't eat dog!

'Even if *T— S—— B——*', said the *Glasgow Herald*, 'is
not a very good play, for the 'prentice hand is in evidence,
it has its moments. . . . The people in the play are types
rather than characters. . . . The development of the play is
too obvious. . . .'

Enough!

Not all the kindly words which were kindly sandwiched
between the sufficiently just observations I have quoted
above (and others which I shall not withdraw from that
baleful envelope) could conceal from me the stern rebuke
I had drawn down on my head by crossing the frontier
without, so to speak, giving up my passport *en route* and
exchanging it for another.

None of that nonsense, my boy! they said to me, and
the warning buzzed in my ear all the way home as I sat in
the restaurant car helping my self-esteem to lick its wounds.
One is either/or and *not* both/and, and woe betide the bold
boy who sees no reason why he should not have a foot
in both camps. To be caught in the cross-fire of no-man's-
land is a chastening experience.

So be it.

Let either/or be the rule; and we are discussing the
'either', the critic, the man who doesn't because he
can't, but who does not hesitate to judge and instruct
and correct and chastise those who can (or think they can)
and do.

The digression is ended.

*   *   *

Your egotistical exhibitionist, untroubled in soul by
any acute awareness of literary values, determined to compete in print as an entertainer with those whose antics on
the stage provide him with raw material, will, if he has
a moderately lively descriptive pen, some good reference
books, and not the slightest qualm about ridiculing

innocent victims who are, like the pianist, doing their best, stand the best chance of attaining a satisfactory degree of notoriety and financial reward. If he has any literary taste and judgement he had better exchange them hurriedly for a sense of fashion—that is much more, as he would say, 'rewarding'. I know one or two such, and the most engaging thing about them is the insouciance with which they plunged into an unknown battleground armed with little more than the will to success and an unshakeable determination to employ any old means (a bizarre wardrobe, an outrageous line in conversation with a stock of carefully rehearsed epigrams, a ferociously sordid affair with a player of curious tastes—anything will suffice) to build up a satisfactory reputation which he will then wear like a dashing opera cloak until the seams begin to fall apart and reveal the ordinary serge schemer inside. One of them began his brilliant career when he came down from his university—where he had distinguished himself by no intellectual brilliance or dogged application but rather by the range and variety of the love affairs which he was reputed to enjoy (reputed, I say, for in sober fact they existed only in the context of publicity material: it was merely the reputation that was desired and not the performance that might nobly win it)—by going without ado to an editor whom I know and informing him that he wished to be, rapidly please, a critic on the payroll.

'What sort of critic?' said the editor, impressed no doubt by the tartan trews which the young person was at that moment, like his habit of throwing in the odd line of homosexual love poetry in demotic Greek, affecting. After all, he had a popular paper to run and this looked like a living gimmick.

'Oh, any sort of critic,' said the young person candidly, 'theatre, films, novels, poetry, television, radio, ballet, chess, art. It does not greatly matter. The fact is that like Sappho:

Οὐκ οἶδ' ὅττι θέω, δύο μοι τά νοήματα

But the important thing is that, as you will have noticed, I have a fundamentally critical, analytical, synthesizing sort of mind and a striking way of expressing what is, if I may without offence say so, a basically interesting personality. It is in my nature to——'

'Quite, quite,' said the editor. 'Quite. What we want on this paper, see, is punch.' He was looking pleased, the old cynic.

'Naturally so,' said the young person, placing in his obscenely-shaped holder (one of Lakhi Khan's cast-offs, dear boy) a black cigarette in which the Macedonian tobacco was mildly mixed with marijuana (a touch of which was all the craze at that moment). 'And I am the man who packs it.'

The job was his.

To deflate him a little the editor sent him off at a moment's notice there and then to Mr Caärd's comedy, *Flensed Folly*, which was playing to packed houses, and requested that a notice should be placed on his desk within twenty minutes of the last curtain. He was back in good time with a notice that began:

'When Mr Caärd was in the cradle an aeon or so ago his nanny used to say to drooling baby-fanciers: "Dinna touch him, dearie, he's that brittle!" The old oracle little knew how her pugnose pet would prove her words true. If you hit a really high note on a fiddle within fifteen feet of him he would shatter like a wine glass. . . .'

But it was when the notice turned to the players that the editor recognized that personal note which later became notorious:

'If I say that Miss A—— is *wallowy* rather than *willowy*, and that is the physical characteristic the part demands if the frail comedy is not to be entirely incredible, I am frank only to be fair. Miss A——, plumping, quivering, jolly Miss A——, would be the first to see, if it were pointed out to her, the funny side of playing the part of a girl young enough (only too clearly) to be her granddaughter. If this production had been arranged in the best traditions of repertory, Miss B——, who plays the maid, and Miss A—— would have changed places. I have never in my life seen a performance so——'

'You've never in your life seen a performance, period, chum,' said the editor, 'but there's hope for you yet.'

There was indeed. Within a few months only, his name was on everyone's lips, thanks almost entirely to his engaging trick of selecting this or that famous actress and abusing her well up to (and sometimes *very* nearly but never *quite* over) the brink of libel.

Per odium, so to speak, *ad astra.*

*   *   *

Well, you dear eager beavers of Oxbridge (and I hope you are paying attention), there is one way to success, and I have no doubt that the more brutally ambitious among you will take a tip from that success story. Get yourself a crew-cut, varnish your finger-nails green, sidle soulfully into the middle pages of *Vogue*, brush up your Shakespeare and de Sade, keep your heads down and bash on.

But do not despair if you are of slightly milder temperament; there are other ways to success in this fevered world. A common method is to graduate through lower forms of journalistic activity such as political or diplomatic reporting, leader-writing, assistant-editing, special-corresponding, gossip-writing, or the like, and have yourself by judicious manoeuvring appointed second-string to some rather over-ripe dramatic critic on an important paper. It should then be quite easy, if you are patient, to intrigue him out of his place ('My dear, of course he's *damn* good, but really, after all, etc., etc.') and move in yourself. You must then quickly decide, if you have not done so already, whether you want to do an Agate, a Scott, a Hazlitt, an Archer, a

Montague, or whatever. The burning of a little midnight oil is quite in order. The great thing is to get your notice written, and all the clever cracks and quotations checked, before you set foot in the theatre. It will only need a little touching up after the final curtain, and then, having delivered it or telephoned it, you can enjoy your high jinks in peace.

If you are of the exhibitionist type, as for the moment I assume you to be, there are one or two points to watch. Make sure that you are always protesting your passionate *love* of the theatre—let it be understood by one means and another that you would simply gasp your life away out of its atmosphere, or *ambience*, as I suppose one ought really to say. In the general theatricality of your clothes, expression, manners, and vices, outdo the most outrageously theatrical player you can think of. Do not, in your writing, be led astray by any twinges of what may appear to be 'conscience', and imagine that you have duties to any other than yourself; dismiss such thoughts firmly and remember that just as an author's text is mere raw material for the producer and players to knock into their own shape, so is their existence mere raw material for the columns which you will with laborious artistry create to your own greater glory.

*   *   *

'But enough of this fooling!' I hear a bespectacled voice cry peevishly. I detect an undoubtedly serious note and so, if the smartypants will excuse me——

There are openings, it is true, for budding pedants. The act of creation is an enormity hard to forgive and it is in the chastising of the creator that the pedant comes into his own with his attitude of: 'Boy; you there; stand up! You have committed a play! How dare you! Such impertinence! Take six of the best!' Everybody knows, or else should know, that the only plays worth seeing are by authors long dead or safely foreign or by Mr T. S. Eliot. The would-be chastiser of the modern theatre must bear this very firmly in mind and make sure that he does not allow any sudden wayward enthusiasm to run away with him. Let him beware of giving praise except, it may be, on occasion to something so inordinately tortuous in form and obscure in content that he can safely assume that no one will understand it. By this means, and others similar, he will keep up his reputation as a 'highbrow'.

First, of course, he must make such a reputation, but this is a less frightening business than one might suppose, providing the candidate has the correct qualifications. Foremost among these I should place a heartily academic temperament; a chip on the shoulder of one sort or another; a moderate hatred of life and all its imperfections and complexities; and a perpetual sense of just anger that so many people should have the insolence, in writing so-called plays, to do indifferently what he himself would do superbly if only he had the time, a room of his own, a private income, or whatever. These will do very well as a basis. It will be helpful if he is a failed scholar of one sort or another for this will ensure an extra injection of bitterness. One should mug up a little theatrical history and amass a sufficient stock of quotations from little known plays of antiquity and from the knottier passages of long dead critics. But above all one should attach oneself firmly to some apparatus of critical theory and to a foreign playwright whose work most successfully embodies it. Every piece must be condemned in greater or lesser degree, regardless of its merit within its own terms of reference, in the light of this theory, and your favourite foreign author may be dragged into the argument as often as you like provided that his work is not well known in this country. In the event of your chosen theory and its best foreign exemplar gaining general recognition here you must immediately drop both and find another pair to take up.

This is not so hard as it seems, for places like Germany, Venezuela, Paris, and Ecuador are immensely productive of *avant-gardes* and you can always find something new to propagate. As to your actual reviews of particular productions, they need bear little relation (if any) to the realities of the matter. If you are a pedantic critic with the makings of mastery in you you will not, of course, care much one way or the other about actors and acting, but since players do seem to be necessary to the theatre, and since their admirers are, regrettably, to be found even among the intelligentzia, you will find it expedient to have something to say about them. A good gambit is to select those who look as if they have a little intelligence (whether they really have or not is a question of small importance) and then write about them as if they were 'intellectuals' whose performances followed some carefully thought out, fully rational plan. They will be flattered by this, and you will be able to write a considerable wordage about actors and acting without knowing the slightest thing about them. Cultivate a stern expression, a distinctive mackintosh, a quarrelsome but quasi-judicial style, and as many prejudices as you can conveniently handle. Travel as much as you can and go to the theatre wherever you find yourself, the boredom of sitting through innumerable performances in languages which you cannot understand is a small price to pay for the impressive data of comparison you can amass. 'Mr Maginty's production of *Bodas de Sangre* is not without its effective moments, but it was hardly to be expected that Shaftesbury Avenue could strike the true high note of *hispanidad* in the centre. I recall Monsieur Hieronimo Scarlatti's version of this moving play at the Théâtre de Mouches de Génève on April 4, 1953, and the uncanny projection of *l'esprit vrai d'Andalouse* which pierced the spellbound audience like a veritable "arrow of song" . . .' That sort of thing. Bags, as perhaps you said during your national service days, of bull. You cannot have too much bull in your side of the business of dramatic criticism, which is indeed, in the opinion of some rather more cynical than myself, virtually nothing else.

★   ★   ★

So much for the two main types of exhibitionist, who would cut their grandmother's throat for a wisecrack. For at this point I must, not without astonishment, acknowledge the existence of dramatic critics whose concern with and for the theatre is more than a mere instrument of egotism. There are, it is true, regions to which the smartypants on the one hand and the sourpusses on the other cannot penetrate; but before our eyes they are dwindling, and I should not like to guess how much room will be left in ten years' time for the intelligent discussion by imaginative men of that damnably absorbing subject, the theatre. Still, for all I know, there may be many genuinely talented young men about who believe that neither the drama nor dramatic criticism is beyond redemption. A word of warning would not be out of place to those of them who see themselves as reviewers. If they survive the passage between the Charybdis of sourpusses and the Scylla of smartypants and emerge with their self-respect intact, their integrity uncompromised, they need not think that their troubles are over and the rest fair sailing. I cannot think of any job in journalism more at the mercy of conflicting winds. Too conscious a fairmindedness can only too readily fossilize into dull indifference. Too conscious a realization of the need to retain the reader's interest leads almost automatically to a forced brightness which is inferior as entertainment to the firecrackers of the exhibitionist who doesn't give a damn for the theatre. Too great a preoccupation with plays of the first rank, or rather with their absence, leads to a silly sort of superiority which condemns everybody for not being Giraudoux or Garcia Lorca or Pirandello. How to balance the play against the performance, the performers against the producers? How to place the production fairly in the lengthening perspective of experience? How to reconcile, within a brief compass, your view of the theatre as it might be (or as you may imagine it to have been) with your knowledge of the theatre as it is? These and other such questions do not worry the talented newcomer so long as he still has something original (or apparently original, for there is nothing new under the theatrical sun) to say; but his stock of originality as a reviewer will soon be used up. Plays are much of a muchness for the most part, and the professional reviewer has to sit in his stall two or three or four or five times a week, looking always at much the same sort of scene, listening always to much the same sort of dialogue. If he did not live always in hope of that unmistakable shock of surprise and exultation which comes when genuine experience is transmitted with the force of poetry, when all the elements of theatre fuse instantaneously into a single formal perfection, when there is no answer to the question: 'How can we tell the dancer from the dance?'—if it were not for this perpetual hope, the occupation of dramatic critic would be altogether unendurable. Even so, with such infinite deserts of boredom to be traversed, not all the aridity can be prevented from entering the soul, and it is always an astonishing thing to me that so few reviewers fall into a numb cynicism of desperation. To the author, the play is unique; to the players, the performance is something into which they pour a large part of their very selves; to the dramatic critic, for all his love of the theatre and its enclosed life, the play, nine times out of ten, is but another shade of grey in a grey kaleidoscope. But this glum vision is one which he must conceal from his readers, and rightly so, for the playgoer who pays for his seat is a great deal closer in spirit than the critic to those whose work he is paying for: and so the critic, if he is to keep his reason and his job, must try to see each of his evenings in the theatre as an individual, fresh experience. So long as the curtain is up he must, in theory at any rate, sit not as adjudicator but rather as common playgoer, emptying his mind of specialist prejudice, preconception, predilection, letting the play-in-performance flow over him as it flows over the most spellbound adolescent in the gods. Only when the curtain has fallen for the last time should he take this experience which he has just been given, compare it with others, dissect it, describe it, pass judgement on it. If he is writing for a daily newspaper he will be fortunate if he has an hour in which to get the job done—more likely, now that the first editions of dailies go to press so early, it will be a case of scribbling something at top speed in a pub and telephoning it immediately to the office. The high responsibilities of honourable journalism are often less important at such moments than the state of one's digestion.

*   *   *

You will certainly end up with an ulcer, young man. That's all that my advice boils down to in the end. Go into advertising instead.

First Night

*

by Ludovic Kennedy

WHEN I was at school, I had two ambitions; to write a book and a play—or rather, to be accurate, to have a book published and a play performed. The first was fulfilled within a few years. The second had to wait considerably longer.

I had, of course, as every would-be playwright does, several practice shots. The first was called *Their Finest Hour* and was a kind of naval *Journey's End*. It was more terrible than tongue can tell; and I cannot look at it even now without sweating with shame and embarrassment. I sent it to Noël Coward (who had said some kind things about my first book) and hoped for an early reply accepting it for immediate London production. The message which finally arrived was a model of tactful disillusionment.

My second effort was rather more worthy, although equally earmarked for oblivion. For a short time during the war I had been A.D.C. to the Governor of an island colony. After the war, when the Socialists were in office, he was succeeded by a Trade Unionist leader, whose salad days had been spent on the footplate. Here, it struck me, was a good situation for a play: the Socialist Governor, well-meaning but inadequate for the job, dedicated never to use force to quell the native riots; the patrician private secretary who had served under and whose sympathies were with the old regime; the Communist son whose sympathies were with the natives, the daughter who hated politics but loved the private secretary, the private secretary's wife who wanted only to go home. I wrote the play and called it *Their Excellencies*. Unfortunately, at almost exactly the same time someone else had almost exactly the same idea. The coincidence was so sharp that for a long time I had an obsession that I had been robbed. This was only dispelled when I learnt that the author of *His Excellency* had himself been A.D.C. to the Governor of Malta: the further news that he was a brigadier put the matter beyond a doubt.

In writing both these early plays my feelings had fluctuated between thinking them original and astonishing creations, and uncontaminated bilge. Mostly, I must confess, I thought the former. Yet in these moments of happy hallucination I had never turned over in my mind what might, or could or would happen between the completion of the script and the glorious occasion of the first night. And even if I had, it would never have occurred to me that everything between these two events would be unpredictable; that what I would have expected to happen would fail to happen, and that other things would happen of which I had not remotely conceived. And yet, when I came to write my next play, that is exactly how it was.

I finished the original version of *Murder Story* in the summer of 1953, and the typescript was delivered to me six days before I was due to leave for a month's holiday abroad. At this moment I considered the play immaculate in every way, and it struck me that the sensible thing was to send it along to Mr Hugh Beaumont whom everyone said was the brightest and best of London managers. This I did, asking with superb impertinence for a decision within five days. There was not a doubt in my mind as to what that decision would be.

Nor was there a doubt in Mr Beaumont's mind. He did not answer himself, but someone in his office sent a reply as prompt as it was unequivocal. Mr Beaumont did not want my play.

I received this letter the day before I left England. It

depressed me beyond measure. It haunted me throughout my holiday. In self-defence I began asking myself who Mr Beaumont thought he was. He was a man who always played for safety, I told myself, his outlook was thoroughly commercial, he had no artistic judgement whatever. And I thought these low, unworthy thoughts with such intensity that I almost began to believe in them.

But as the weeks and months went by and the play was rejected, as monotonously as faulty bottles in a glass works, by one management after another, my mood began to change. No, it was not Mr Beaumont's judgement that was at fault, it was my own. No, it was not a very good play I had written, not even a competent play: it was, let's face it, a thoroughly bad play. I believed this with just as much sincerity and conviction as I had originally thought it a masterpiece and Mr Beaumont off his head not to accept it. (The truth of this matter is, I think, that no play is ever as good or as bad as its author imagines it.) Finally, towards the close of the year, I put the play in a drawer, forgot its existence, and turned my attention to something else.

And there, but for a chance encounter, the manuscript might have remained to this day; for if the first moves in this extraordinary game had been unlike anything I had expected, the next was even more so. Some months later Mr Michael Benthall, the Director of the Old Vic, and Mr Robert Helpmann came to dinner to discuss with my wife the new production of *A Midsummer Night's Dream* in which she and Mr Helpmann were to tour America. I had known Michael Benthall since schooldays at Eton where I had played Horatio to his Hamlet (Dennis Cannan, I remember, was the ghost). During dinner the fact that I had written an unsuccessful play came out in the course of conversation. Mr Benthall asked if he could read it. I resisted this request, not from any false modesty, but because by this time I believed sincerely that the play was barely worth the paper it was written on. But Mr Benthall was importunate, and at the end of the evening took the manuscript away with him.

I met him again at dinner two or three weeks later. He liked the play, he said, but the last two scenes were quite out of context with the rest. I saw at once the value of this criticism, went home and rewrote the last two scenes, and sent off a revised version to my agents. A fortnight later I heard that Mr Warren Jenkins would be producing the play in six weeks' time at the Cambridge Arts Theatre.

This news left me quite stunned, for at that moment I had no means of reconciling my own opinion of the play with the (presumably) contradictory opinions of Mr Jenkins and the Cambridge Arts Theatre. In any case it all seemed too good to be true. And it was. We had forgotten about the Lord Chamberlain, and that princely character wanted certain things altered. His representative, a charming soldier, told me about these in an interview in which he also expressed his own views on hanging; and this, by way of footnote, was about the only predictable thing I can remember happening.

By the time the corrections had been approved, it was too late for Mr Jenkins to produce on the date planned. Mr Norman Higgins, however, of the Cambridge Arts Theatre, said that he wished to put the play on at a later date. The wish turned out to be stronger than the deed. For the whole of that spring and part of the early summer Mr Higgins and I carried on a gay flirtation. Twice we made assignations for a betrothal and twice something came between: on the second occasion I was obliged to give way to the obviously more endearing charms of the Guildhall School of Music.

A few weeks later Mr Peter Haddon swam over my horizon. No wooing was needed of him: it was love at first sight. An early marriage was arranged at the Hippodrome Theatre, Aldershot. There was to be a reception afterwards to which householders on both sides of Shaftesbury Avenue were to be cordially invited.

The pattern of the next six weeks was, oddly enough, much as I had imagined it. A producer was secured, and a cast, and rehearsals were started in a bare room above a public house in Soho. We progressed in an orderly manner from day to day. As I watched the actors at work I became aware of a sensation which I suppose is common to all playwrights; that of the play, which for so long had been my property alone, passing out of my keeping and into theirs. We moved from the room in Soho to the stage of the Cambridge Theatre, from the Cambridge Theatre to the Hippodrome, Aldershot. And there, one warm night in June, the play had its first performance.

The reception was encouraging. *The Times* and the *Guardian* had some nice things to say the next morning, and the London managers were polite, if reserved. I knew that more of them were coming later in the week, and, hopeful that one would, in his own good time, consider a West End production, I left for a fishing holiday in the north of Scotland. Here unpredictability sprang its biggest surprise. Less than a week after I had arrived in Sutherland my agents telephoned to say that, after a two weeks' provincial tour, Mr Tom Arnold was bringing the entire production to London.

Although recent events had caused me to alter my own opinion of the play, I had never regained the blind unquestioning faith I had originally had in it. But from now on I felt encouraged to do so. There was the undeniable fact that a London management considered it worthy enough to bring to the West End. The notices in most of the Birmingham newspapers were what are known as 'raves' (one man called it another *Journey's End*). The *Evening Standard* asked for first refusal of the serial rights (they had serialized only two plays since the war—*A Streetcar Named Desire* and *Death of a Salesman*), and by the morning of the first night had the first two instalments set up in proof. Finally, on the same day, the *Daily Express* sent along Mr John Barber and a cameraman to take a series of exclusive photographs.

(Needless to say neither the serial nor the photographs ever appeared.)

Nor did this snowball end with the first night. The applause at the end of the performance was loud and long. I cannot say how many curtain calls there were because I lost count. There were cries of 'Author' (the nursery dream come true) and after a decent pause I gave a hasty little bow, nearly precipitating myself into the stalls in the process. Afterwards a number of theatrical people congratulated me with the same curious phrase. 'It looks', they said, 'as if you've got a success on your hands.' I mention all this because I am not a regular first-nighter, and I did not then know that the favourable atmosphere which can build up round a play and be generated through the theatre on its first night is no guide at all either to its merits or its life.

The play had opened on a Thursday, and a week later, confident that it had settled in for several months (a view which one or two critics had expressly stated) I left London for a few days in the country. Here came the last in the series of unpredictable happenings. Late on Saturday night I received a message that the advance bookings were so bad that withdrawal notices had been posted, and the play therefore had already had its last performance. I spent a bewildered twenty-four hours trying to assimilate this news. On Sunday evening I received a further message that the withdrawal notices had been cancelled, and the play would continue as planned.

It did, in fact, continue for a further six weeks. In retrospect I see it would have been a miracle if it had lasted longer. It had opened in the middle of the summer holidays, its theme was mournful, its cast unknown, and it was playing in a theatre situated among side streets. I have since been asked why I allowed the play to open when, where, and as it did. The straight answer to that is that, having sold an option on it, I had no say in the matter. Yet even if I had I think I would have held my tongue; for such considera-

tions carry little weight with an author whose first play
has been offered a definite London engagement.

In any case, by the morning after the first night, I had
come to view the play with a certain indifference. My
own work on it, my own part in it, had ceased (apart from
a few minor alterations) on the day rehearsals had started.
I have mentioned that on that day I was aware for the first
time of my losing possession of it. This feeling grew in
intensity until, by the first night, I had the curious sensation of watching a play with which I had little connexion,
which almost seemed to have been written by someone
else. The night the play was, so to speak, born, was the
night for me on which it finally died. I was obliged to go
to several subsequent performances, but it required an
effort to do so: my mind was on other things.

The novelist has some knowledge of what will befall his
manuscript: he will receive galley proofs, page proofs and,
in due course, the completed book: his sales are likely to be
between two and ten thousand copies. The future of the
playwright's script is, as I hope I have shown, less predictable. I am, at this moment, finishing a new play. I do not
know whether it is good or bad; but I am constantly buoyed
up by the thought that, other things being equal, the
chances of its running for six months or alternatively never
seeing a stage at all are about even.

and here is a passage from the First Night play in question—

Murder Story

by Ludovic Kennedy

Murder Story *directly attacks capital punishment. Were you to meet Jim Tanner, he would strike you on first appearance as a lost twenty-year-old youth whose mind had never developed, but as you grew to know him better you would realize that behind his vacant stare, monotonous expression, his lack of confidence and inability to settle down and lead a happy life, there were his inner thoughts which were constantly present in his mind, trying, but failing, to understand. . . . He is a misfit. Alone and backward, different from his other schoolmates, he was never able to master reading or lessons; now he is an equal failure at trying to keep a job for more than a few days. He is an impressionable lad, able so easily to be led astray in the wrong company. And when one day he allows himself to follow a bait of money which has been held out to entice him to take part in a robbery, he does not realize the consequence until all is too late. For things go wrong and the youth he is with loses his nerve, pulls out a revolver, and he watches a policeman fall. He does not try to defend himself when he is put on trial for his life. In the cell he has an opportunity, through the help of the chaplain, to reconstruct the parts of the debris of the world which he never understood and which collapsed upon him. He would be able to come to terms with living if only he had a second chance. But it is too late. Here is a passage between Jim and the Chaplain, who gives him the courage to die 'like a man'.*

[JIM *sits down at table, and* CHAPLAIN *joins him.*

CHAPLAIN: You weren't expecting much from the appeal, were you?

JIM: No. Not after what you said. Still . . .

CHAPLAIN: It comes as a bit of a shock, doesn't it?

JIM: Yes.

CHAPLAIN: The reprieve's the thing you've got to hope for now.

JIM: Do you think I'll get it? The Governor said I might.

CHAPLAIN: I think you've got a very good chance. Better than average. Your parents have started a petition for you, you know. They've got several thousand names already.

JIM: Do they know? About my appeal? Mum and Dad, I mean.

CHAPLAIN: Your mother knows. I was speaking to her a little while ago.

JIM: Is she here?

CHAPLAIN: Yes. She's coming to see you shortly.

JIM: And Dad?

CHAPLAIN: He's not here today.

JIM: He and Mum always come together.

CHAPLAIN: Look, Jim, you've probably heard the old phrase about bad news coming together. Your father's not too well.

JIM: Oh!

CHAPLAIN: He's had a slight relapse. Nothing serious. But the doctor doesn't want him to leave the house. Not for the present, anyway.

JIM: Poor old Dad. Is Daisy coming?

CHAPLAIN: I'm afraid not. You see, she's had to go out to work.

JIM: But she's having a kid.

CHAPLAIN: I know. But things aren't too easy at home, Jim. There's not much money coming in.

JIM: Oh!

CHAPLAIN: So your mother's got a lot to worry about. Your father. Your sister. And you. She'll need a bit of cheering up.

JIM: Yes.

CHAPLAIN: I think she's going to find seeing you this afternoon a little difficult. And you're the only person who can help make it easier. Do you think you can do that?

JIM: Yes. Yes, I will. I'll try.

CHAPLAIN: Good boy. I hoped you'd say that.

JIM: It's all my fault, isn't it? What's happened to Mum and Dad. If I hadn't gone that night, they'd be all right. Wouldn't they?

CHAPLAIN: Yes, but you weren't to know that. You mustn't take too much of the blame. [*Pause.*] You know Jim, you've changed a lot since you've been here.

JIM: How do you mean?

CHAPLAIN: Well, before you were all shut up in your shell. Didn't like anybody, didn't trust anybody. Now you've opened up, come out of your shell. You're like a different person. Don't you feel it yourself?

JIM: Yes.

CHAPLAIN: I wonder why?

JIM: Everyone's been very good to me. No one's ever been so good to me. They've treated me . . . well, as though I mattered. Made me feel I *was* someone.

CHAPLAIN: And so you are.

JIM: Yes, but I'm scared though. I'm ever so scared.

CHAPLAIN: About what may happen?

JIM: Yes. I wish I knew. It wouldn't be so bad if I knew.

CHAPLAIN: Have you thought about what we've been talking about these last few days?

JIM: You mean God and all that.

CHAPLAIN: Yes.

JIM: Yes, I've thought about it a bit. But I don't think I quite understand.

CHAPLAIN: Well, let me put it this way. Do you think you'd be less frightened if you knew—knew for an absolute certainty—that someone was waiting for you?

JIM: Yes, I suppose so. But there couldn't be . . .

CHAPLAIN: Why not?

JIM: Well, there just couldn't be. Not if you was dead.

CHAPLAIN: But there is.

JIM: How do you know?

CHAPLAIN: I don't *know*, Jim—that is, I can't prove it to you. It's just something I feel. And hundreds of thousands of people feel it too. And if you feel a thing long enough and strongly enough, then in the end it becomes true—and you *know* it's true.

JIM: I'm sorry, I don't understand.

CHAPLAIN: Do you remember the bit I read you from the Bible about how God made the world?

JIM: About Adam and Eve and all that?

CHAPLAIN: Yes.

JIM: Yes. It was a nice story, that. I liked that story.

CHAPLAIN: And you believed it, didn't you? I mean, you believed it really happened?

JIM: Yes.

CHAPLAIN: Well, then, doesn't it strike you as reasonable that if God put people into the world, He's waiting to see them when they come out of it again?

JIM: Yes, I suppose so. I'm still scared, though.

CHAPLAIN: Everybody's got to die sometime, Jim. Every single one of us.

JIM: Most people don't know when.

CHAPLAIN: Oh, but a great many do. Sick people. Old people. I've seen them.

JIM: Ain't they scared?

CHAPLAIN: Some of them are. But not those who—put their trust in God. I've never met anyone who was frightened of death who really believed in God. They're almost—glad. You see, they know they're going to a happier place.

JIM: What's God like? What's He look like?

CHAPLAIN: Different people see Him in different ways. Nobody really knows, because nobody's ever seen Him. Many people think of Him as a very old man, a very kindly old man with a long white beard—rather like Father Christmas.

JIM: Father Christmas! I like that. Do you see Him like that?

CHAPLAIN: Yes, Jim, I think I do.

JIM: And He's waiting for me?

CHAPLAIN: Yes, He's waiting for you.

JIM: You wouldn't kid me?

CHAPLAIN: No, Jim, I wouldn't kid you.

JIM: How can I be sure He's waiting for me?

CHAPLAIN: You must try and get near Him. The nearer you can get to Him, the easier it'll be.

JIM: What do I do?

CHAPLAIN: Talk to Him. Tell Him your thoughts. He won't answer you—at least, you won't hear anything—but He'll be listening to you all the time. And, Jim, you must pray to Him. Have you ever prayed?

JIM: No.

CHAPLAIN: Would you like to?

JIM: All right.

CHAPLAIN: Well, kneel down with me. [*They kneel.*] That's right. And cross your hands. Like this. Now say this after me. [THE CHAPLAIN *says, and* JIM *repeats, line by line, the following:*

   God be in my head, and in my understanding,
   God be in my eyes, and in my looking,
   God be in my mouth, and in my speaking,
   God be in my heart, and in my thinking,
   God be at mine end, and at my departing.

JIM: That was lovely.   [*They get up.*

CHAPLAIN: I thought you might like it. I've typed it out on a piece of paper so you can say it when I'm not here. [*Hands* JIM *paper.*]

JIM: Thanks ever so. I could spell it out with my letters, couldn't I?

CHAPLAIN: Yes, of course. And I'll bring you another one later.

JIM: Oh, thanks.

CHAPLAIN: I'm going to leave you now, Jim. Think you'll be all right?

JIM: Yes, thanks.

CHAPLAIN: Your mother'll be along shortly. Don't forget what I said.

JIM: No.

CHAPLAIN [*moves towards door*]: So long, Jim.

[*Exit* CHAPLAIN.

[JIM *takes the piece of paper over to his letters and starts spelling out the prayer. Enter* GRAVES *and* BARTHOLOMEW. *When they see what* JIM *is doing, they stop suddenly.*

JIM [*reading*]: God. Be. In. My. Head. And. In. My. Under–standing.

[*There is an eager, happy expression on his face. He reaches forward for the first letters.* BARTHOLOMEW *and* GRAVES *watch him as*

THE CURTAIN FALLS

CAUTION:—This extract from the play *Murder Story* is fully protected. The play is published in an acting edition by Evans Plays, Montague House, Russell Square, London, W.C.1. No performance of this play by amateurs may take place without a licence having first been obtained from the publishers. For all rights other than amateur apply Margery Vosper Ltd., 32 Shaftesbury Avenue, London, W.1.

Art Theatre or Show Business

*

by John Fernald

WHEN THEATRICAL journalists write of 'the English theatre' they get round the difficulty of defining it by drawing distinctions of quality. They will compare the West End theatre with the better provincial repertory theatres, because both do much the same kind of play; they will bracket the Old Vic with Stratford-upon-Avon, and the London Arts Theatre with the Lyric Hammersmith for similar reasons. The distinctions they draw are rough and ready, based on the quantity of capital available for the presentation of 'good' productions. They will often disagree about quality in a play, but they will usually be unanimous in thinking that the more money there is behind a presentation the better the production will be. Plentiful backing, they assume, means better sets, better actors, better producers and even better plays.

Up to a point the assumption is a true one. But it is only a half truth; it leaves out of account a factor that makes the production a living thing—that mysterious complex of impulses which drives producers and actors to create a theatrical performance. Distinctions of quality are not concerned only with economics, nor with the individual merits of the actors. They depend equally on how far these impulses are controlled by the actor's own integrity, and how far they are misdirected by other and alien forces. It is the theatrical artist, whether he be writer or actor or producer, who makes the theatre live. It is his integrity and his power which preserves it in the perpetual battle that goes on within it. That battle is concerned with artistic values: economics play a part, but their importance is really secondary; ability also plays a part, but ability can fight on either side—for it and integrity are not the same thing.

The conflict is between the theatre of truth, which may or may not justify itself at the box-office, and the theatre of show-business, which is an equally chancy business and is the only theatre which most managements can understand. The battlefield is the public, mostly inarticulate and unaware, an easy prey to surface values, ready to be led anywhere when leadership is forthcoming.

To complain of show business in its proper place is a waste of effort. It has always been with us and it always will be. Nobody need object to spectacular revues, ice-shows, Hollywood films and other manifestations of popular relaxation—provided their currency is recognized for what it is. But when that currency circulates in the legitimate theatre it debases all values there: and the danger of false values is a constant challenge to the artist. Today false values abound. There is the notion that personality and acting are the same thing—an idea born in Hollywood and fostered by our films, our television and our commercial star system. There is the belief that comedy cannot be serious and that tragedy cannot be comic. This is ingrained in the heads of theatrical journalists (despite the work of most of the great dramatists who are put in a category by themselves as exceptions to the rule). There is the notion that the theatre must always 'take one out of oneself', ignoring the fact that no human being can escape from himself except into a prison of his own making. Such notions, believed by many managements, aired by many newspapers, are easily accepted by a public conditioned to take what it is given. They are the notions of show-business, and should be confined to show-business. If allowed to spread they could destroy the theatre, for the theatre's strength lies in its power to create reality: once superficial effect is allowed to supplant reality the theatre becomes no different from the other kinds of show-business—except that it is not so efficient and far more expensive.

Left to himself the theatrical artist can usually meet this challenge. It is from him that the vitality of the theatre springs. The curious longing to express the truth of life through his technique gives him an integrity which is almost unassailable. He is menaced only when success drives him into a theatrical climate where the values of show-business dominate his work. It is then that the existence of the 'Art' theatres becomes important: through these he can keep his standards bright even if they have become tarnished from time to time in the course of earning his bread and butter.

The 'Art' theatres, that is some of the better repertories and the London Arts Theatre, are theatres where policy is mainly controlled by the artists themselves. In them the standards of the actors are embodied in a producer of taste, skill and experience, whose ideas, intelligently modified by economic necessity, are allowed to express both his and his company's artistic aspirations. This does not mean that they exist in a rarefied atmosphere of Art for Art's sake unaware of the importance of the box-office. It does not mean that some of the plays they do will not turn out to be bad. But it does mean that whatever plays they present will be performed because those who produce and act them are able to look upon the task with excitement and joy. A sense of adventure, of discovery, of humility towards himself and respect towards his material, above all a love for whatever side of the theatre his talent calls him to— these are the qualities the artist brings to his work.

The showman does not understand such feelings: they are not in his nature. He and the artists he employs each speak a different language. A measure of the difference between them is the low status of the producer in the West End of London. Most actors can tell a good producer from a bad one with remarkable unanimity, but their opinions do not always coincide with those of the theatrical manager, who may be guided in his choice by considerations not of merit but of whether a producer is pleasant, easy-going, and, most important, tactful with stars. Whether or not a producer's sympathies, background and experience make him suitable for the play chosen for him is not a question with which a manager is often troubled. Consequently, in the West End, complete harmony between producer and play occurs more by chance than design. When it does happen, the chance of the harmony extending to producer and cast is problematical, for, as like as not, the company will be chosen by the manager, not the producer. They will be chosen to make a suitable background for a star who will himself be the reason for the play being put on at all. The producer will find that his ideas must all be slanted to suit his star's requirements—and these requirements can result in a travesty of what was the intention of the author, since many stars have long lost their early zeal for serving an author in humility. Films have often emphasized their personality-appeal for so long that they have forgotten how to characterize: tricks alone have become their stock-in-trade. The producer who tries to break them of these tricks will be in difficulties: he will get no support either from the stars or the management since both have come to believe that tricks are what the public want to see.

When a company has a star like this at the top of the bill the effect upon them is insidious. When a supporting player finds that a 'laugh' that is properly his own affair is being lost through the cunning manoeuvres of a star, he promptly schemes to get his own back. In no time the business of putting the play over has become a battle of wits and the actors a band of unco-ordinated jugglers. Ultimately the company's faith in itself is lost, and the personal regard of each of its members for the others: the play and its author are forgotten.

To the mass of the public all this may not matter. Show business has distorted their values, and they are star-crazy. But any theatre-lover who has seen good plays produced at

K

Birmingham, Bristol, Liverpool, or the London Arts Theatre, and has seen what has happened to them when re-produced by a West End management with a change of cast, will have recognized that something, sometimes a great deal, has been lost in the process. There is a satisfaction in watching a fine team, more lasting than the thrill from most virtuoso performances. A company bound together in mutual regard and respect, with a producer who leads but does not command, can demonstrate a precision and delicacy of interplay which is infinitely exciting. Such a company needs a fine play, and fine plays need such a company; it is not surprising that nowadays those authors who can afford not to write for show-business are looking to the Arts theatres to perform their plays in a manner that will not leave them disillusioned. The existence of what Mr Norman Marshall has called 'The Other Theatre' is something for which to be profoundly thankful. Without it, the theatre as a true expression of life would cease to be.

The Cinderella of the Muses

*

by Lothian Small

TO COME upon beauty anywhere is a joy. If it is
found in a foreign field and stirs in the finder an urge
to transpose it into his mother tongue, the joy may then be
still more widely shared. To translate anything of a beauty
or truth so compelling calls for the artist's touch; it can also
produce a new work of art. Yet that seemingly did not occur
to the people who most enriched our western culture. And
our most satisfying translator today in his chosen field of
the Greek classics, Dr E. V. Rieu, has an explanation. He
holds that the Greeks of that age were too busy exploiting
the beauties of their own language, too contemptuous of the
'barbarian' tongues around them, to bother about translation or look on it as an art at all. From that he goes on to
show that, throughout the long history of criticism, translation has been the most neglected of the arts—the Cinderella
of the Muses.

That will seem the more surprising if we stop to ask
one question with a fairly obvious answer. What proportion
of our knowledge and wisdom, whether for use or delight,
of the sciences, pure or applied, of the history, philosophy
and law, of the religion, drama and poetry of all civilizations
has come to the majority of us through the medium of
translation? Very often, too, it comes through translations
of translations, with all the possibilities thus involved of
distortion, which will vary with the capacities, the conscience and the standards of the translators. The end
product may therefore be at many removes from the
inspiration of the original work, may, on the contrary,

capture it with genius (sometimes even improving on it)
or be on any level in between.

An excellent instance, both of our debt to translation
and of some consequence of the way it was done, is to our
hand in the great book of Christendom, the Bible. How
many of us reading the English Authorized Version realize
its varying debt to Hebrew, Greek or Latin? We ought to
remember as well all that authorities in this field attribute
to the happy accident that Tyndall, to whose earlier text
that version is so indebted, was one of the rare scholars
of his time to know Hebrew. It was he therefore who,
while his confrères were making their transfers out of
Greek and Latin translations, was carrying straight across
into English a great deal of Hebrew imagery, much indeed
of the very vocabulary and phraseology which we now
feel most native to our English ear and soil.

Just as translation brought the Hebrew strand in that
way into our inheritance, so it was with those from ancient
Greece and Rome. The power of the impact of that Greece
upon generation after generation, seen through a translation like Chapman's *Homer*, Keats expressed for us all
when he eased his heart of love and wonder in the lines:

> Then felt I like some watcher of the skies
> When a new planet swims into his ken.

In similar ways we have come to know and assimilate
many another new planet of the mind. And in every age,
as knowledge grows and habits of thought and feeling as
well as their expression change, the need is felt to have
rendered anew in the idiom of the age literature which,
however old it may be, has values that endure. With *Homer*,
Dr Rieu has done this for us today, his renderings of the *Iliad*
and the *Odyssey* allowing us to feel almost at home in the
air of that earlier world, to become young again.

Holding that in the *Iliad* we hear the Tragic Muse for
the first time and that the *Odyssey* is the true ancestor of

the novel, the translator felt that his problem was to present in mid-twentieth century English this 'first expression of the Western mind in literary form'. Intending his version to be genuine translation and not a paraphrase, he did his best, he says, within the rules he had set himself, 'to make Homer easy reading for those who are unfamiliar with the Greek world'. In that spirit he does not hesitate to bring a twinkle to the eye as when we hear Circe quoting Keats to Odysseus: 'the goddess only cried out at me as an obstinate fool, always spoiling for a fight and welcoming trouble.' 'So you are not prepared', she said, 'to give in even to immortal gods! I tell you, Scylla *was not born for death*: the fiend will live for ever!' With the same free delight an image lifted straight out of Fitzgerald's paraphrase of eleventh-century Omar Khayyám's *Rubaiyát* comes here from the lips of Homer's Hyperion, when he calls on Zeus to punish Penelope's suitors for slaughtering Odysseus's cattle: 'They had the insolence to kill my cattle . . . that gave me such joy every day as I climbed the sky *to put the stars to flight.*'

Such translation is certainly the 'easy reading' its writer aimed at. Incidentally, the two phrases italicized further show—as comparable gems from the Bible and other classics could—how a translator can coin or give fresh currency to a phrase which then becomes legal tender at any place or time throughout the commonwealth of letters. But vocabulary, with its idioms, was not the only problem confronting the translator of the *Odysseus*. If his version was to be well received today, he could not leave it to speak for itself. It had to be properly introduced, and much of the sixteen-page introduction is devoted to making Homeric religion clear to modern Christendom, since Homer 'regards his gods, though immortal, as made in the image and likeness of man'.

Does translating a modern play, we may ask, raise comparable questions? Does it differ inherently from translating the classics, or are there principles or problems more or less constant whatever the period and languages involved? In the most systematic review I know of the subject of translation in general, by Dr Rieu in 1953, he arrives at what he calls 'the principle of equivalent effect', meaning, with certain provisos, that the best translation is the one 'which comes nearest to creating in the audience the same impression as was made by the original on its contemporaries'. From that principle follow two important corollaries: first, if the original was intelligible to its audience, intelligibility should be the translator's first aim; second, that, in turn, means writing in contemporary idiom unless the original was deliberately archaic. No translator could wish his aim or his achievement rated higher than that; creating the same impression, an equivalent effect; and in the review mentioned that criterion is applied critically to the major translations into English. Further, when we are dealing, not with works separated from us by centuries and civilizations, but with works of our own age, say a play written in one and translated into another language of Western Europe, with so much of common cultural inheritance, we can better evaluate whether the equivalent effect is achieved. That point, and the first corollary about the intelligibility of the original will now be considered.

It is not generally realized—and by those who know no language but English it is hard to realize—that our mother tongue, so very rich in countless other ways, has today one disadvantage which sets it apart from practically every other. It is the fact that it has dropped out of its currency the second person singular pronoun 'Thou'; and it is no good saying with Anglo-Saxon insularity 'Who wants to *thou* anybody nowadays?' For most other peoples are doing it all the time, and we just can't translate them when they do. The Germans distinguish clearly between the *Du* used automatically between relatives, friends, comrades and colleagues at school or at work, and at once or nearly so between persons of a similar social and professional standing meeting for the first time, and the more formal *Sie* form of address. In other languages, mainly non-European, the 'thou' is always used, I am told, when addressing a single person and the plural reserved for a speech aimed at two or more people. In French, the use of *tu* is not basically different from the German one but much more restricted, with the result that *tu* indicates either close family relationship, real friendship or—between man and woman—intimacy, although quite recently the *tu* has become more common between fellow students and friends of the opposite sexes. The French even have the verb *tutoyer* meaning to address somebody as thou. Yet the equivalent does not survive in English except in prayer, perhaps among Quakers of the old school, or when a young lady is told: 'I'll sing thee songs of Arabie in ye olde English.' Everywhere else, children, playmates, workmates, members of a profession, of a team or (with many subtle nuances) of a family *thou* each other, and relationships can be deliberately, even dramatically changed, by switching from the familiar 'thou' to the formal 'you' or the other way round. The whole social temperature can thus rise or fall and that change of atmosphere can rarely be rendered in English. It is therefore not the translator but our language today that is to blame for the impossibility of getting equivalent effect in translation wherever the 'thou' form of address is used.

That difficulty baffled me for a long time in the first play I ever translated, the *Eurydice* of Jean Anouilh. There the point is concentrated in a short French text which will repay close examination. The moment comes in that play, it may be recalled, when Orpheus, perplexed by Eurydice's verbal contradictions and an inarticulateness he cannot understand, needs absolutely to believe that she now is true to him in word and deed. He overhears recrimination between her and the gross impresario Dulac who had blackmailed her into becoming (only to save a weaker being from getting the sack) his unwilling mistress. They

are using the word *tu* and Orpheus wants to know why.
Here is the French:

EURYDICE [*to* DULAC]: *Tu* peux rire, je *te* connais, *tu* ris
jaune.
ORPHEUS [*to* EURYDICE]: Pourquoi *tutoies-tu* cet homme?
EURYDICE [*to* ORPHEUS *in utter sincerity*]: Mais je ne le
tutoies pas.
DULAC [*sneeringly to* ORPHEUS]: *Vous* voyez? Et le reste est
à l'avenant, jeune homme. Je *vous* dis que *vous vous*
égarez.

What does that crucial passage amount to? Eurydice
addressing Dulac uses the *tu* or *te* three times. Orpheus,
dreading it means she is his mistress, asks why she does.
Eurydice answers that she doesn't, which is true and false—
true in so far as she is meaning Orpheus to know that she
does not love Dulac but is only using the regular theatre
jargon, false in being a flat verbal contradiction. The
point to grasp here is the dramatic emotional effect produced by the laconic French text. Poor, perfectly sincere
Eurydice feels she has put herself in the wrong, is the more
terribly alone, and having got fankled in her words has
flung solidly together against herself the man she loves
and the man she loathes. The best English expedient I
could think of is this:

EURYDICE: You may smile, my dear, I know that sickly
smile.
ORPHEUS: 'My dear!' Why that familiarity? Some understanding between you?
EURYDICE: Oh, darling, there is and there isn't.
DULAC: You see. And that's her through and through,
young man. You're on the wrong tack, I tell you.

The only thing saved in that rendering comes from the
question 'some understanding between you?' which allows
Eurydice to answer with the useful English expression,
'there is and there isn't'—that in turn letting her explain

that she was 'thou'-ing in the way of all theatre people, not of a woman to her lover. But it is laboured, the pre-fabricated *trouvaille* has none of the spontaneity of the original dialogue, and the French audience can follow, in a way denied to the English, the mounting tragedy of the misunderstanding between Orpheus and Eurydice.

Quite a different kind of difficulty arises in tackling a text like that of Claudel's *Partage de Midi*, included in this book, difficulties both of matter and form, substance and style. The fault might well be the translator's, did not many French admirers of the author also find the original hard to grasp. After all, that an author who is so polished and self-conscious a stylist should nevertheless not always be highly intelligible at first is not such a paradox. For this diplomat scholar—steeped both in the Bible and in the Greek classics, disciple of Aristotle and Saint Thomas Aquinas, and 'illuminated' (his own word) by the 'Illumina-tions' of Rimbaud, before gleaning, while translating Aeschylus and Pindar, material that served him as ex-ponent and practitioner of the art of poetry—developed a style which was labelled by detractors *Claudélien* and judged wilfully and unprofitably artificial. With Dullin, and less amiably with Copeau, he had discussed the dramatic language of his own plays, dwelling on the supreme signifi-cance of the consonants in stage speech. What then must be the shoals, the overtones and the ground swells which the translator would look out for in such an artist's writing!

Besides that, Claudel was a devout Roman Catholic who had thought long and deeply of entering the priesthood but, try as he might, had heard no call. He was theologian and philosopher, anthropologist and cosmologist. In youth he had suffered a devastating experience from whose effects he only got deliverance in writing *Partage de Midi*. This four-character play hinges on a twofold theme, that of adultery and that of the conflict between the religious vocation and the call of the flesh. For the author the characters—the husband, Ciz (who from natural causes and with dramatic aptness lies in a Hong Kong cemetery by the second act), his wife Ysé, her lover Mesa (a man denied the religious vocation) and their friend Amalric— are all symbols, which some will be able to decipher in reading the closing scene. But if ambiguities remain and if the translator cannot find from the context whether or not the author (who has proclaimed elsewhere that the physical and the metaphysical merge) has reached in his thinking a life-giving synthesis of body and spirit, or whether for him they remain hostile entities poles apart, translation must inevitably at times veer toward interpretation. Two confessions made by Claudel in discussions of his life and work with Jean Amrouche, broadcast in 1948, are illuminating on this point.

In those conversations, when comparing the original published version written about 1905 with the one very much adapted indeed and played by Jean-Louis Barrault and his company in December 1948, Claudel deplored much of his earlier imagery in such passages as that in Mesa's hymn:

'Je vois l'immense clergé de la Nuit avec ses evêques et
ses patriarches.'

Such passages Barrault, on the contrary, greatly admired and wanted to keep for the stage. The second admission was about the rôle of Mesa himself which, Claudel recognized, was not 'quite in focus' in his own mind—surely reason enough for an uncomfortable feeling in French readers and for guess-work by a translator! Further, the author submitted to Barrault four amended texts in succession, from the first three of which bits had been transferred, with insufficient harmonizing, to the stage text already in rehearsal. When the fourth, about which the author felt happiest, was submitted, he accepted with the best grace possible the producer's refusal to change yet again. The stage version published in 1949 bears Claudel's dedication: 'To my excellent interpreters of the Théâtre Marigny,

Edwige Feuillère (Ysé), Pierre Brasseur (Amalric), Jacques Daqmine (de Ciz) and Jean-Louis Barrault (Mesa) who was, besides, a marvellous producer. Thanks to him it was possible for *Partage de Midi* to be played for the first time in Paris.' Nevertheless, English or American actors or producers interested in an English production might be well advised to consider along with this one the earlier more poetic version.

Should the two kinds of difficulty, illustrated here in *Eurydice* and in *Partage de Midi*, seem to have been unduly stressed, this much more may be said. The first, due to a deficiency peculiar to English since we dropped the 'thou' form of address, is one of which no reader of a translation in English who knows only that language, could be aware except through some such explanation; further, the demonstration was attempted in the context of an important modern French play at a point in its emotional and dramatic development where the original atmosphere, the savour, *le ton qui fait la musique*, simply cannot be conveyed in English. The second difficulty, extreme unintelligibility or ambiguity in an original, was examined in a foreign play from which one of the longest extracts in this book is taken, *Partage de Midi* of Paul Claudel, whom many English critics pronounce untranslatable.

That charge, made here about Claudel in particular but not peculiarly applicable to him, occurs in English criticisms in sweeping statements like 'French is untranslatable' often enough to raise the general problem of the frontiers of translatability—a problem concerning both subject-matter and its translator. A distinction drawn by Pope between the literature of knowledge and the literature of power goes to the heart of the matter. It is further developed by De Quincey in a passage which, though dealing with books to read, applies no less to plays that are to be seen or heard. He wrote: 'Books, we are told, propose to *instruct* or *amuse*. Indeed! . . . The true antithesis to knowledge, in this case, is not pleasure but power. All that is literature seeks to communicate power; all that is not literature to communicate knowledge.'

So far as subject-matter is concerned it is a safe generalization that works which only communicate knowledge, that is, the factual, ponderable matters—the kind to which De Quincey denies the name of literature—can be translated from one into any other language having counterparts in institutions, techniques and vocabulary. Secondly the work of translating can here be done by anybody who has adequate command of the second language, whether it be his mother tongue or not. In that other category, the literature of power, where the main data are different in kind, one generalization, this time about the translator, is again possible; only in the rarest cases can a translator transpose work of this kind into any other language than his mother tongue.

In the literature of power, the field proper to drama, where the raw materials are the imponderables of human motive and action, other laws than those of knowledge operate. For as soon as the mind moves from fact to feeling, from ponderables and concepts which prose can carry to the emotional and imaginative borne on feeling, which in any language has its own rhythms and native idioms, then different experiences are impelling the writer and, through his expression of them, his readers, hearers, observers, communicants. The artist's work of power has a unity making it different in kind from the thinker's construction. Thus, a clause in the middle of a treaty or a sentence descriptive of current events can be translated without much reference to context, or to clauses coming before or after, by people familiar with the vocabulary and conventions; it can even be translated identically by different people similarly equipped.

But a speech or a bit of dialogue occurring well on in a play is a wholly different matter and begets, or ought to beget, a different attitude in a translator. A seemingly factual statement may be charged with emotional significance the more eloquent for its verbal austerity. It cannot be equivalently rendered without knowledge of earlier or later words and situations in which the character is involved, or without intimate appreciation of the author's intentions. It thus may mean choosing between several possible adjectives or other qualifying words or phrases, variously able to convey the development in character, plot or feeling secured by the author's use in the original of particular words at that particular place in the economy of the play or poem as a whole.

Even so, another problem sometimes confronts the literary translator. The more expression tends in any language to imagery, the wider the range of interpretation possible. If that is true for people of the author's own language, it must apply still more to his translator. If, further, even the author's compatriots find the original in whole or in part incomprehensible, condemn it as verbiage, camouflaging ill-digested thought or, more generously, as a groping towards ideas or values still not clear within him, the translator may have to cope with problems as much ethical as linguistic or aesthetic. Ought he, for example, to make the translation, if he can, a better, more coherent work of art than the original? My own principle is that, since *le style c'est l'homme* or 'manners makyth man', it is the translator's duty to enable his readers to appreciate for themselves the style as well as the gist, not only what an author says but also how he says it.

How many translations, published or played, reach the standards there implied? Apart from a few outstanding exceptions, the proportion of really good ones which reach publication or the stage in America, Britain, France or Italy is low indeed, while many which get there do a great disservice to Latin-Anglo-Saxon understanding. To their credit, it is true, many publishers issue worthy English versions, although many more—with deplorable results—have inadequate supervision of work apparently farmed out like repetitive piece work at so much a thousand words.

With some firms the translator must fight to have his name given due prominence, to have rewards as high as those of unskilled labour or any share in royalties, however much or long the success of his work may profit the publisher. Thanks, however, to the combined efforts of a few agents of courage and integrity and a few enlightened publishers, the situation is definitely improving. Similarly, in the theatre we can boast of brilliant producers doing wonders with good translations which also reflect credit on the management—even at times with bad ones which do not. In the field of dramatic criticism too, by no means all the critics are linguistically equipped to assess the translator's part; yet that part can reflect or distort the author, render his creation sympathetic, antipathetic or colourless to the audience and so influence English feeling about the mental climate and the people of its country of origin. Those critics, however, who know the original language do increasingly acknowledge the translator's contribution— even if he is not a T. S. Eliot or a Christopher Fry. But the disservice done to an important side of our international relations by those theatres, publishers and others who, however unwittingly or unwillingly, give bad translations their wide diffusion today is a blot on our cultural landscape calling for reform. Until we 'reform it altogether', the imputation of our mental slovenliness in this field, so often heard abroad, will be justified. So long, in the English-speaking world, will literary translation remain the Cinderella of the Muses.

Why work in a field so full of risk, we are often asked, and what are the rewards? This glance at one experience may serve others as a warning or a challenge. If I entered the field by chance, it is after a fairly full, though unplanned preparation. Plays and poetry, theatricals and languages had always attracted me. During my university years at Glasgow (which overlapped with Bridie's) that great man of the theatre, Alfred Wareing, enabled us to see the first English performance of *The Seagull*, Granville Barker and

Lillah McCarthy in *Man and Superman,* and other really great acting.   Relations in international life afterwards with men and women of many tongues were not without their touch of the dramatic and poetic, although the urge to translate such things came a good deal later.

During the war the London weekly *France* once printed Jules Supervielle's *France malheureuse* and *Prière à l'inconnu,* poems crying out to come into English.   Obeying the urge, sending my versions to the author and considering them with him in his Passy home after the war led to a valued working friendship.   Similar friendly working relations with Aragon, Eluard, Reverdy, Tardieu and others produced a fair amount of English verse renderings.

Drama came unexpectedly.   Being in Paris while Anouilh's *Antigone* was on at the Atelier, I went, saw and was conquered for translating for the stage.   Captivated by *Eurydice,* I first translated that.   Then Anouilh handed me an English version of his *Medée* with a remark that brings us back to our central theme: '*Mon Anglais est nul; mais je n'y trouve pas mes cadences.*'   He was right, not only were the cadences lacking (the thing a poet hears in any language), but all the poetry and passion of the original.   Work with other playwrights followed, from the veterans Cocteau and Vildrac to younger ones; including Bour, Cesbron, de Beer, Druon and Dutourd.

What rewards can the translator expect?   Today, anything from a net loss to a fortune.   The literary translator does not live—any more than other artists, it is true—in a social or economic vacuum.   But whatever the rewards, his profession does not have too many skilled practitioners and needs more of the right kind.

Television and the Theatre

*

by Isabel Quigly

TELEVISION is an instrument. In time it may produce a new art-form, but that time has not yet arrived. Nor is it primarily a medium for dramatic entertainment. It seeks to entertain, yes; but does so in a score of ways, most of them unlike those we would normally call entertainment; and, most important of all, its concern is daily life. In the theatre we see only the play: the weather, the government, football results, are all left outside. In the cinema we see, apart from the news-reel, only the films we have chosen. Daily life again is left outside. But television reports and comments, gives advice, instruction, and criticism, on our daily way of living. You can call it, for lack of a more specific word, journalism; and certainly television as it is today in this country is far nearer in spirit to a newspaper than it is to the theatre and the cinema.

Instead of reading, you watch; but its time is divided, like the space of a newspaper, between the things that newspaper readers expect to find. It deals with news, features of every kind, sport, politics, personalities, education, travel, women's interests, children's interests, hobbies, accomplishments, and straight entertainment. Some of its programmes are frankly labelled 'magazine programmes'. Like a newspaper, it bears in mind that some of its public likes gardening, some cooking, some country life, some urban; like a newspaper it occasionally runs competitions, sometimes answers questions, often invites its public to contribute to a particular section, and always welcomes its public's views. Again like a newspaper, it comes into its own most spectacularly on a great public occasion, in which, through it, the public can take part, and with which, though remote, it can identify itself.

Within this large range of topics, entertainment as such—a show, I mean, designed for none of these journalistic reasons—has a relatively small section of its own. And of this small section, in which I would include variety, dancing, concerts and recitals, and the popular parlour games, a small subsection is the business of the drama department. A small section of a newspaper may be given over to a short story or an imaginative article, and to the literary reader it may appear the most interesting thing in the paper; but to the editor it competes for space and attention with gardening notes and the stock market.

Television's main function, then, is not dramatic but journalistic: to be a kind of strip-newspaper, where what is normally described in writing can be watched in action. But, unlike a newspaper, it cannot subdivide its public, and aim at a particular part of it. Unlike the radio, too, it has no division, at least as I write, between Home, Light, and Third Programme tastes. It is as if readers of *The Times* and the *Daily Mirror* had all to share the one newspaper at breakfast.

Such a state of affairs will continue only until there is more of a choice of programmes in this country. At present, audience and programmes interact in a circular movement. The audience influences the choice of programmes, which in turn influences possible viewers of the future; with the result that viewers tend more and more to come into similar categories of taste. In answer to a questionnaire sent out recently by the *Spectator*, it was found that of 7,000 readers only 13·9 per cent. were television viewers; and Mr Angus Wilson, in an article on class distinctions addressed to the upper middle classes, writes, as a suitable question for determining the social level of one's friends, 'Are you really glad you haven't got television?' To assess the tastes of millions, particularly in drama, is a formidable

L

task for anyone; and the outraged indignation which may greet any experiment in the choice of plays might well encourage the drama department into a timid mediocrity. But this is a condition which a choice of programmes, and therefore, from the producer's point of view, a certain choice of audience, should do away with. At present the audience is too large, too various, for the producer to know quite whom he hopes to address.

And to know whom you are addressing is the essential of every medium of entertainment: to gauge the quality of the audience; its understanding, intellectual or sympathetic; its mood while watching; its whole state of mind. When understanding is lacking between entertainer and audience, things look as they did to a child I heard describing an advertisement to her mother: 'There's a blob of green on a long line of white, and squiggles on it.' (It was a flag, with the name of the product advertised written across it, on a flagstaff.)

*   *   *

Because in each case a performance, an audience, and a frame round the performance is involved, television, the theatre, and the cinema have all been rather arbitrarily linked. Enormous differences of technique and yet larger differences of intention divide each one from the others; but the most basic difference that I see between television and the other two, the difference, too, on which the development of television as an art and particularly as a dramatic medium depends, is a difference in the audience. In the theatre the producer, in the cinema the director, is addressing a crowd, a crowd gathered in a special building to enjoy a common experience. On television he is speaking to individuals, and individuals in their own homes and in everyday surroundings.

Both the theatre and the cinema make the mere fact of going there a little, as Mr Salteena would have it, less mere; it becomes, quite apart from the play or the film itself, something of an occasion. The decorations, the lighting, the furniture, the music, all play up the differences between where you are and the rest of the world. The very effort made to go there, when you might have stopped dully at home, sets the evening in some way apart. But the greatest influence is in the rest of the audience, in the fact of seeing, breathing, laughing, feeling, with hundreds of others.

The responses of the theatre differ, of course, from those of the cinema. In the theatre there is the essential and incalculable *rapport* between audience and actors; in the cinema emotion goes out from an audience to actors who are far away, for emotions felt long ago, for a performance edited, sometimes out of all recognition of the original, by the director. But in both the feelings are *shared* feelings, there is the enormous vague presence of those other hundreds in the dark, the strange electric proximity of others through which (it is hardly far-fetched to say) currents of emotion can quickly pass. A crowd has its own life, its own responses and personality, quite distinct from, and at times even at variance with, the individual responses of those who comprise it. There is a collective, as well as a personal, emotion, and it is on this, as well as on the individual response, that the theatre and cinema play.

A matinée performance in a three-quarters-empty theatre, an early afternoon showing of a film in a deserted cinema: these are experiences quite distinct from the normal experiences of theatre or film going. A dramatic performance on television (I am trying to avoid the word 'play' with its too theatrical connotations) is something quite different again. For the audience consists of one, two, three, at most a small group; and the viewing takes place without effort, without preliminaries, almost without much expectation, in familiar—the most familiar and ordinary—surroundings. The response of the audience is prosaic, critical; it is almost entirely individual. Unrestrained by the thought of disturbing two dozen neighbours, people comment; unexalted by warmth, glamour, and the company of hundreds of their fellow-beings, they are sharp-eyed, in a debunking and deflationary mood. You can put things across, get away with things, when a man is outside his home that you cannot get away with by his own fireside. And since most television is viewed in a family atmosphere, it is worth remembering that exaltation is generally harder to kindle and sustain within the family than without.

If it is wary, the television audience is also, paradoxically, a more intimate one than that of the theatre or the cinema. Though an audience of millions, it is individual and personal to an extraordinary degree. It is both closer and more remote than theirs; it watches something both 'live' and unalive. The actors, it is true, are photographed, not flesh-and-blood people as they are in the theatre; yet the audience watches them in action, at a continuous performance, not, as in the cinema, one edited and served up months later. There is the immediacy of the present, the intimately noted and uncorrectable actions of people who yet, it has to be admitted, are not in fact there; not in the flesh, not in the room. Yet the actor speaks to each one of his audience, his message is direct, his effect is on the single viewer, not the group. It is as if he were playing in millions of homes, all separate, yet all of them intimately involved in what he does.

*   *   *

Utterly different though it is from them both in intention and effect, technically television drama has hovered, until now, between the theatre and the cinema. The plays chosen are as a rule plays written for the theatre, and even those prepared specially for television still accept the conventions and the limitations of theatrical production and of a theatre audience. A certain mobility, but very little, is possible. This means that the sets used are merely slightly enlarged and elaborated stage sets, with staircases, angles, and nooks of all sorts, with the possibility of peering

round corners and going through doors, but without any
of the wide mobility of the cinema, or the enormous sweep
from an immeasurable distance to a microscopic view of
mouth, eyes, or hands.

In other television programmes the audience is accustomed to the long shot of the cinema, to the landscape and
the speed of movement possible when television is reporting
events outside the studio. When a show is frankly taking
place in the studio—as happens, for instance, in the case
of panel games—there is no feeling of restriction, for no
imaginative effort is required with the scenery, and no
cinematic conventions have been invoked. But when a play
is televised with sets only slightly larger, movements only
slightly less restricted, than those of the theatre, the feeling
of cramp may become acute. The present extremely low
standard of design in the B.B.C. television sets may be
partly responsible for this—sets as a rule of a hopeful but
appalling realism that misses the realist's one quality, and
the point of his existence, that of being at least life-like.
But there is more to it than poor design. There is the
inability to realize television's basic differences from the
theatre, the inability (it appears at least so far) to think,
except timidly, in television's own terms.

A new medium needs above all pioneers to use it, to see,
before it has been developed, its own peculiar and till now
unthought-of possibilities. The cinema found them. Early in
its life directors appeared to experiment with the new medium
in other terms than those of its dramatic predecessors. The
early films occasionally show an over-theatrical gesture,
a voice still unused to conversational level, or an eye too
heavily made up, as if for the stage. But not often. Even
before they understood it fully, the early directors took the
film on its own terms, delighted to explore the vagaries and
virtuosity of its behaviour. Before it, most men's eyesight
had been restricted to their own level. They saw things
strictly from a man's eye view. 'Why has not man a microscopic eye?' said Pope. 'For this plain reason, man is not

a fly.' The cinema gave him his microscopic eye; and not only the fly's view but the eagle's, the aeroplane's, the galloping horse's, the express train's. It enlarged and diminished his vision to degrees till then undreamt of. It placed him, like Gulliver, among giants or Lilliputians, the height of a blade of grass or tall enough to survey a world.

It is thus, by bringing its audience into more intimate touch with its subject than ordinary eyesight could have brought it, and at the same time enlarging immensely its range of vision, that the cinema compensates for its lack of flesh and blood. Were it merely a photographed play, comparison with the theatre would enter into it and the absence of solid actors become intolerable; it would have the limitations without the life of the theatre. And this is almost exactly what happens with television plays as they are produced at present.

The individual producer is not at fault: he is working to impossible requirements. First of all he needs what few men have, an equal experience and ability as film director and theatrical producer. For his eyesight is the camera, but his actors, unlike film actors, are almost immobile in their one or two small sets because acting through a continuous performance. He needs the theatre producer's ability to handle them through this continuous performance, to mould them to an (uninterrupted) interpretation of his views; but he lacks the film director's power to reshape the performance to his own wishes and in his own time. He needs the film director's technical knowledge, though it can at best be creakily applied, to handle and make the most of his cameras. And because the continuous performance is the antithesis of the film, as the photographed and distant performance is the antithesis of the theatre; because the director (to use film terms) cannot set his mark on what is happening when the camera's movement is restricted entirely to the consecutive movements of the actors; and because the long shot, and even the full close-up, can be only rarely and gingerly used, theatrical and film instincts must be always at variance, the producer and director constantly quarrelling in the one man.

This unsatisfactory state of compromise, for which there seems, if drama production on television is to continue on its present lines, no remedy, may explain why no one in the first rank of either theatrical production or film direction— no Olivier, no Orson Welles—is at present working, at least regularly, on television drama in this country. Such a man might enlarge the possibilities of what appears a very restricted form of dramatic production; but it seems un- likely that he would be attracted by so unrewarding a medium, because from the producer's point of view it would appear to have almost no intrinsic value at all. Tele- vision drama will certainly continue to exist as long as there are people who 'like a play', and prefer a poor substitute for the theatre to no theatre at all; but it cannot be said to offer any artistic challenge either to the theatre or to the cinema. A commercial challenge is another matter, but if television can be said to draw crowds away from the theatre, the cinema, and even the pub, it must be remembered that, except during a very small proportion of television viewing, it is not television *drama* that is doing so; it is televised sport, interviews, talks, news, discussions, variety, and documentaries of every sort; it is the weather forecast, Big Ben, and the announcers: all the journalistic elements I mentioned earlier.

It cannot, I think, be overemphasized that television presents no *dramatic* challenge to the other forms of enter- tainment. Its techniques are not theatrical, its effects on the audience (I have tried to show) are not like those of the theatre. Most of those who have been outstandingly successful on television have not even been professional actors; at any rate not well-known professional actors. Occasionally, even, professional actors fail disastrously on television, for the very reason that their theatrical technique will not stand up to the unfamiliar atmosphere and condi- tions of television. These television failures are generally not intimate, humdrum, 'throw-away' enough for such a medium; they frighten, with a 'performance', the unprepared-for-it parlour. Television can use nothing larger than life-size, even on a great occasion; even then it must humanize the grandeur so that it does not strain the parlour walls or the parlour's very limited credulity. It is not so much a case of stretching the domestic limits as of making the outside world small and homely enough to fit them.

Those who have done well on such programmes as the panel shows, or the announcers whose names are household words, whose personalities are those of family friends, whose weddings sell out the evening papers—these are all *television* phenomena, not actors; people who have understood the essentials of television behaviour. I use the word 'behaviour' instead of 'acting' because, skilled though they may be in projecting their television personalities, their success is just that of personality, of a single and immutable personality—their own. They are not required to act in the theatrical or even the film sense of the word. They are simply required to *be*; to be, in each case, themselves, and if the self happens to please, they are successful.

*   *   *

Where will television drama go from here? There are two general possibilities. One (which is what I imagine will happen) is that plays will continue to be produced with the outlook that at present exists: that is, with the same notion that a play can, with the help of a few cinematic techniques, be transferred lock, stock, and barrel from the theatre. Development in that direction can, it seems to me, be only in the matter of detail: acting more suitable to the medium, a smoother pace or a more interesting rhythm, a more recognizable and personal style of production, and, let us hope, a higher standard of design. But the basic artistic insufficiency of the present form of drama production will remain, the present uneasy and invalid compromise between other, and valid, forms of production and techniques.

This kind of drama, besides giving pleasure to an enormous number of viewers who cannot or would not get to the theatre, has no doubt an incalculable educational value in introducing plays of all kinds to people who would never before have seen or perhaps even heard of them. Naturally it is doing well if it is only increasing love of the legitimate drama (though reports of which plays are most popular with television audiences are not encouraging). But good advertising is not necessarily good art. I once saw *Tess of the d'Urbervilles* as a strip cartoon in a French magazine, which might quite legitimately have claimed to be spreading a knowledge of English literature about the provinces of France. There is much to recommend our television drama on moral but less on artistic grounds.

The second possibility is that television will develop the alternative forms of dramatic entertainment that it can do very well: forms which exploit television's need for the individual, the direct, the personal approach and response. Story-telling does admirably on television; the single face speaking in close-up can be extraordinarily dramatic, and, if the personality is right, needs no movement or illustration. Solo performances of most kinds do well—dancing often comes across excellently, and musicians and their instruments are always photogenic—so that recitals of any kind are good: poetry spoken, even recitals of dialogue, anything in which movement outside the speakers is not necessary. For those who want a story told, and actors acting it, films would seem a better solution than the present one: either ordinary commercial films if they were obtainable, or, better still, films made specifically for a television audience. Documentaries, half acted, half factual, do very well on television as it is; and television can take a bigger dose of facts and figures than most mediums of entertainment.

Television's sociological importance raises frowns, eyebrows, and attention; its artistic possibilities, its suitability or unsuitability for particular forms of production, seem almost ignored. For ten years now it has been feeling sociologically important in this country; its influence, though not its prestige, is undisputed. A television *mystique* would appear rather comical; but some plain thinking, at least in the drama department, some decision on what is television and what a hodge-podge of theatre and cinema, would seem apt, if not urgent, today.

The Eyes Have It

*

by J. A. Wilson

THE CINEMAS of Britain attract as many people in a
week as do the theatres in twelve months. That is one
of those little-known—although, when you come to think
of it, not surprising—facts that must, I believe, preface any
comparative discussion of film, theatre and television.

What is the explanation of the cinema's hold on twentieth-
century man? Why do movies in our time attract intellectuals as well as day-dreaming adolescents? Why is it
that, at its best, the cinema is the most effective synthesis
of the popular arts of our time?

The answer, I think, lies not so much in the content of
what we see and hear in the cinema, but in the nature of
film-going itself. Films appeal to the Adam and Eve in all
of us: they bring us together in our shared emotions. The
theatre no longer does this for the mass of the people.

James Bridie once said that the one immutable Law of
Drama was that it must succeed in making the spectator
unconscious of the passage of time: if a play does this, it
fulfils its function and has merit. Other qualities of a play—
its educative, its thought-provoking, its exciting, its poetic
qualities—are not basic. The important thing—the way
to achieve this desirable theatrical state—is to have a
complete rapport between the actors and the audience. That
is something that does not exist in the cinema, and when we
find it in the theatre we realize there is nothing quite like it.
It is theatre's golden key. Fundamentally, all that is wrong
with the drama today is that this rapport no longer occurs
as often as it should. In the things that our dramatists

choose to discuss, we no longer see with the same eye and spirit. And we must do that—tinker, tailor, soldier, sailor, rich man, poor man, beggar man, thief—if the theatre is to be truly popular.

In the cinema it is different, and I think it might be useful to analyse and explain that difference.

The psychologist, Hugo Mauerhofer, observed some years ago that one of the main symptoms of what he called the 'cinema situation' was the most complete isolation from the outside world. From this he deduced—what any film-goer could have told him—that the ideal cinema would be one where there was absolutely no source of light except the screen itself, and where not even the faintest noise, other than the sound-track of the film, could penetrate. The reason, he said, is that sights and sounds, other than those that seem to come from the screen, remind us of the outside world, and that is something we want to avoid.

Two interesting, and observable, psychological effects follow from this. The darkness of the cinema induces an incipient feeling of boredom and at the same time sets the unconscious to work. The film that appears on the screen meets both the incipient boredom and the keyed-up imagination. Immediately, says Mauerhofer, the roused imagination takes possession of the film, which records a specific action on the screen by visual means: at the same time, the changed sense of time creates a desire for intensified action. With very few exceptions, it is intolerable to watch a story recorded on the screen at the same pace as events would occur in reality. All of us, in the cinema, feel a subjective desire for a concentrated form of film narrative. Unless this desire is satisfied, our feeling of boredom, so far dormant, will inevitably reawaken.

Incidentally, it is interesting to note in this connexion that, although film has been put to different uses in different parts of the world, recognition of the truth of Mauerhofer's observation is world-wide. Ilya Ehrenburg called the film 'a factory of dreams', and when the anthropologist,

Hortense Powdermaker, turned her attention to Hollywood, she, too, called it 'The Dream Factory'. While in sleep we ourselves produce our dreams; in the cinema they are presented to us ready-made.

Here again the point can be illustrated from personal experience. It is a fact that for some time after leaving a cinema the state of mind of the film-goer is changed, and this change is apparent to an outsider. With people of strong imagination and considerable repressions, the effect of film experience can be observed in their attitude, gait and gestures as they come out of the darkness into the light.

All of this is unlike anything the theatre can offer. Dreams are for the secret heart, and the cinema provides the dreamer with privacy. In no other public place, and certainly not in the darkened theatre, are we subjected to such anonymity as in the cinema.

These psychological elements—namely, the boredom lurking continually on the edge of the film-going experience, the increased liveliness of the imagination, the uncritical, voluntary passivity, and the anonymity which guides the spectator into his most private sphere—these are the mainstays of the 'cinema situation', in Mauerhofer's belief.

His conclusion is that the part played by the film in the life of modern man can hardly be over-estimated. 'It originates from its peculiar psychological conditions and the extraordinarily wide range of its influence, in many cases increased by the modest intellectual demands on the film-goer, who, indeed, has simply to follow his eyes and ears.'

This, then, is a psychological explanation for the power of the film—and I think a convincing one. But I would suggest that there are equally impressive biological reasons for the cinema's dominance as a public entertainment. We all know that as sensory organs our noses are very poor. Our ears are fairly good, but our eyes are our principal sensory organs. The visual sensitivity of the human brain compared with that of the animals is, I am told, enormous.

The growth of the visual penetration of the brain developed
pari passu with the dexterity of the human hand. It is
because film and television appeal to our eyes, and because
our eyes are more important than our ears, that these visual
media have such a grip on so many of us. When you add
to this the special circumstances of the cinema's presentation, you have, I submit, the true explanation of the film's
power and influence.

*   *   *

Television, as we have noted, makes the same appeal to
the eye as the cinema—but in very different circumstances.
There will always be forms of entertainment that are best
enjoyed either in flesh and blood or at least in the 'night-
out' atmosphere of a public place. The intimacy of the
home cuts two ways. Obviously, television does have
special properties, but it is likely to wait a long time before
it finds an aesthetic. To me, as to Isabel Quigly, it is like
journalism: all we can reasonably ask for is honesty and
good grammar.

The French film director, René Clair, has said he believes
that the special virtues claimed for the 'live' element in
television are spurious artistically. I believe this to be true,
and if I may add to the observations already made by Isabel
Quigly I would say that one of the first impressions one
gets in a television studio is a sense of speed. The television camera has an even more insatiable appetite for
material than radio's microphone. You simply cannot
spend time in describing something that the camera 'sees'
instantly. The next impression is of unbroken continuity.
There can be no pauses and no 'retakes'. Third, and perhaps
most impressive, is the sense of the audience just beyond
the control panel, watching and listening to everything
that comes within range of the camera and microphone.
The feeling is almost that of facing an audience directly,
even though its reactions cannot immediately be felt.

The rapidity, the necessity for a continuous line of

action, and the consciousness of the audience make working
in television like drawing an artist's sketch while people
look on, rather than creating, as in film, a mosaic made up
of hundreds of carefully matched little pieces fitted together
in accordance with a large preconceived design. In films,
changes and rearrangements are always possible, but in
television the final decisions must be made at a speed
requiring almost instinctive judgement by one man.

Clair, as I have said, claims that it is an illusion to make
this purely technical property of television its chief artistic
merit. Television, he claims, has nothing unique of its own
to give as a medium of dramatic expression; it is merely
another means of exhibiting films. Moreover, Clair claims
that if the film had been invented after, and not before,
television, producers of plays on TV would have seized
upon it at once as a device to free them from the impossibly
clumsy task of putting a visual production directly on to
the air.

Roger Manvell, one of our most perceptive critics, tried
to counter these arguments in a series of articles published
in this country, and the point he made is central to the
argument I am putting forward here. As I have said, I
agree with Clair in so far as he is speaking of the drama.
But there is a gap in his logic, and Manvell spotted it. The
Frenchman's arguments, he said, seemed to neglect one of
the most important factors in the practical development of
any branch of story-telling (dramatic or otherwise): the
point of view of the members of the audience.

'A novelist', said Manvell, 'is catering for an audience
made up of solitary individuals who can take up or put down
his book at leisure; the dramatist has to deal with a theatre
full of people whom he has got to keep in an active state
of attention to what is going on. The audience at a film
knows that space and time are at the control of the film-
maker, and consequently they expect the suppleness of
narration which the medium allows: they also know that
the players in front of them are shadows, and that what they

see and how they see it depends finally on the skill of the film-maker in presenting carefully preselected moments in the acting of the artists. The excitement, therefore, lies just as much in the way the story is presented as it does in the quality of the acting.'

I think Manvell's first point is well taken, although I suspect that the awareness he attributes to his audience is present only in a comparatively few people. The rest, I would say, neither know nor care about the technical background which makes a film (or a play or a television show) possible.

The point, though, is that television reaches a very large audience, the members of which may be expected to react as individuals rather than as masses of people. This seems to call for a slower, quieter technique than is necessary in a film. Certainly, in this country, television drama has been more nearly home theatre than home cinema. The intimacy of television provides the opportunity for a link between individuals difficult to achieve in the cinema.

If I may recapitulate, this article began by referring to the much greater hold the cinema has over its public than the theatre. This, I contended, was not so much because of what people saw in the cinema, but because of the physical conditions, and the psychological consequences, of film-going. I take the accepted view that the prime fact of television is 'the instantaneous and complete transmission of actuality', but agree with Clair that this 'live' element is meaningless artistically. Aesthetically, I don't see that we need fear for the future of theatre or cinema. Television will certainly not kill them, although it may be that many theatres and cinemas will close down. Television will become one of the primary means—perhaps *the* primary means—by which people get their entertainment, their information, their mental stimulus, and their experience of the world. It is going to do for the cinema what the cinema did for the theatre: teach it to mind its own business.

Ideally, cinema and television will present strongly

contrasted forms of entertainment, working as partners along with the theatre. Film and TV will have the mass audience because, as I have tried to show—the eyes have it! The theatre will never have the immediacy of television, nor the hypnotism of the movies. It is as well, I think, that this should be faced. What is left is exciting and magical enough. There is no substitute for the living drama.

M

It is Midnight, Dr Schweitzer

by Gilbert Cesbron

translated by Lothian Small

The curtain rises on DR SCHWEITZER, *who is alone, sitting at the piano playing Bach. Throughout the Act will be heard the chirp of crickets, animal cries and mysterious calls. The characters should, without over-emphasis, make the spectators feel that the night heat is overpowering. In his shirt and white linen trousers* SCHWEITZER *plays for a moment with his back to the audience.* MARIE, *in nurse's uniform, comes in by the door right, with letters in her hand. She is beautiful but with the beauty of roses beginning to tire with too much sun. She goes to the piano, listens for a while and at last speaks.*

MARIE: It is midnight, Dr Schweitzer.

SCHWEITZER [*gives a jump, turns to her, bows in greeting, returns to his playing, then speaks without turning round*]: In my Alsatian home, Mademoiselle Marie, it is only six o'clock. From the Gunsbach belfry the Angelus is sounding, and my little daughter stirs in her sleep. . . . An angel is passing overhead.

MARIE [*firmly*]: Here it is midnight and time you were in bed.

SCHWEITZER [*getting up*]: Very well. But while the sun sets here, it is watching still elsewhere. [*Sitting down again, he suddenly asks in a kind of anguish.*] Listen! Is this all right still? [*He plays a passage of Bach.* MARIE *listens and nods.*] Sure?

MARIE: Yes.

SCHWEITZER [*Stopping and pivoting round on the stool, he faces front. Looking at his hands he speaks quietly.*] The hands of a woodcutter, a carpenter. . . .

MARIE: Of a great surgeon.

SCHWEITZER [*as if he hasn't heard*]: No longer the hands of an organist.

MARIE [*brusquely*]: What about me? Have I any vestige of looks left?

SCHWEITZER [*stupefied*]: But. . . .

MARIE [*quietly and bending her head*]: Have I the looks of a woman? Any grace?

SCHWEITZER [*getting up abruptly*]: You are feeling sorry you. . . .

MARIE [*sharply*]: I am not!

SCHWEITZER [*excitedly pacing up and down*]: Yes, you are. Sorry you decided to leave. You must go back to Europe, Mademoiselle Marie! Yes, yes! I shall never steal one minute of anybody's time. . . .

MARIE: Doctor, I assure you. . . .

SCHWEITZER [*going on as if speaking to himself*]: The value of a single minute is not the same for any two human beings. The time of a beggar who must die tomorrow is more precious than mine a thousandfold.

MARIE: He doesn't realize it.

SCHWEITZER: No more do I. That is why the time of any-body else—of everybody else—is sacred. Promise me, Mademoiselle Marie, that if ever. . . .

MARIE [*smiling*]: Your time too is sacred . . . and it is past midnight.

SCHWEITZER: For one moment then let time stand still, —a few more bars of Bach. One blessed moment! May I, please? [*He plays. In a moment a tom-tom is heard in the distance. MARIE who has noticed it first, goes and opens the double doors. The sound comes clearer. SCHWEITZER stops playing, gets up, listens and interprets.*] Child . . . child sick. [*The tom-tom stops.*] A sick child. But I missed the beginning of the message. We must get everything ready. There will be people coming. [*He looks at her for a moment in silence and then says gently*] You seem unhappy tonight. . . . [*Silence, then sharply*] Let us work! [MARIE *goes through the letters she had placed on his desk.* SCHWEITZER *goes to a table on his left, picks up a carafe and a glass.*] Some fruit juice?

MARIE: No, thank you. [SCHWEITZER *sits down, putting the carafe and glass on the desk.* MARIE *has opened the letters. She tells him, one by one, the contents.*] Strasbourg University asks when you are going back. [SCHWEITZER *makes a vague sweeping gesture.*] They say they are keeping your Chair vacant for you.

SCHWEITZER [*with an effort*]: Tell the Rector he musn't . . . that I am never going back. [*Speaking as if to himself*] Me make a career? That is over and done with. What else, Mademoiselle Marie?

MARIE: Your publisher has had nine requests for the translation rights in your books on St Paul . . . he asks you——

SCHWEITZER [*interrupting vigorously*]: Let him do what he thinks best. I trust him. Next?

MARIE: Seven requests for organ recitals from . . . [*Taking the letters one by one.*] Edinburgh . . . Stockholm . . . Amsterdam——

SCHWEITZER [*breaking in*]: For next winter? [*She nods.*] Accept them all. We need money. [*He gets up and looks at the hospital plan on the wall.*] I want three more huts before the summer of 1915. . . . Maternity, minor surgery, mental.

MARIE [*handling the rest of the letters*]: Here's the very thing . . . donation . . . donation. . . .

SCHWEITZER: Whatever should we do without our friends in Europe?

MARIE [*irritated*]: Say rather, what would our black friends do without us.

SCHWEITZER: As you please. What matters is that each of us gets the help he needs.

MARIE: As I see it, some give their money, others give themselves!

SCHWEITZER: As I see it, some have a bad conscience and others a carefree smile.

MARIE: Much the same thing.

SCHWEITZER [*sharply*]: No! Because you are not smiling. . . . Come along, what is wrong?

MARIE [*rising, goes to the main door at the back*]: I feel as the forest does, as all Africa at nightfall, when it is waiting for the storm. I am stifling.

SCHWEITZER [*going to her*]: The storm is over now, the leaves revived, the earth has drunk deep and the trees feel refreshed to the core.

MARIE [*sotto voce*]: Happy trees!

SCHWEITZER: Tomorrow morning, silently, the sun will begin torturing them again. Africa, its thirst unslaked, will be stifling. But you will not. You will have work to do again and will forget the dreadful night. [MARIE *sits down again.* SCHWEITZER *watches her and then says as he takes a glass of fruit juice.*] A bit too highly strung for this climate.

MARIE [*half smiling, half aggressive*]: Aren't you, Doctor? Look, you have just upset your fruit juice . . . you see. . . .

SCHWEITZER [*smiling*]: I did it on purpose.

MARIE: Whatever for? [*Suddenly getting up.*] Listen! [*In a second she turns towards him, abashed.*] I thought I heard. . . .

SCHWEITZER: That is Africa. One is always thinking one hears. It's what you don't hear that is really dangerous. Go and get a good sleep, Mademoiselle Marie.

MARIE: No . . . not tonight . . . I couldn't.

SCHWEITZER [*smiling*]: We tell stories to children who are too excited to go to sleep. What story can I tell you? I've got it . . . my first case . . . the night we arrived. The sick man lying on top of two packing cases in the hen-house there, transformed into an operating theatre . . . the oil lamp smoking . . . my wife, who was helping me, was trembling.

MARIE: Trembling?

SCHWEITZER: Yes. For out of the darkness the whites of eight pairs of eyes, glued to us, were following every movement I made. Eight M'fan warriors armed and feathered like fighting cocks.

MARIE: And the operation was successful?

SCHWEITZER: Otherwise we should not be here now. The job I did that night defeated all the sorcerers of the great forest! The news was spread during the night by tom-toms. By dawn canoes were arriving in shoals. Whole families. As soon as they reached the landing-stage they started to shout their new nickname for me... N'tchinda...

MARIE: N'tchinda?

SCHWEITZER: The man with the magic knife.

MARIE [*after a pause*]: What nickname would you give me?

SCHWEITZER [*smiling, but serious*]: Baloua la. [MARIE'S *eyes ask the meaning.*] The woman who has not yet decided.

MARIE [*in a colourless voice*]: Have you cures for the soul, too, Dr Schweitzer?

SCHWEITZER [*slowly*]: Here is one which has kept me going until today—my fortieth birthday! I have never believed it necessary to be what people call 'reasonable'.

MARIE: What?

SCHWEITZER: In my youth I swore I never would. When I heard grown-ups talk of their earlier ideals and enthusiasms it sounded as if they were children who had died. It terrified me to think I might one day be like them. So I resolved to go through life with a clear conscience.

MARIE [*slightly ironical*]: And that brought you happiness?

SCHWEITZER [*after a moment's reflection*]: It is dead of night in the depths of the bush ... and you and I are alone. Yet I am loth to confide to you a truth it took me years to admit—there is no such thing as happiness.

MARIE [*almost shouting*]: I don't believe you!

SCHWEITZER: It is a truth one learns, but does not teach.

MARIE [*same mood*]: Well, I am sure that happiness exists.

SCHWEITZER [*imposing*]: Very well, but whoever deserves it knows he has no right to it, but must shoulder his part of the world's burden of pain. ... [*Pause.*] So he renounces happiness for a fuller, more life-giving joy.

MARIE [*violently*]: And it is life-giving joy to leave his wife and his only child in Alsace? Leaving his parish behind, a Chair at the University and the certainty of becoming the foremost organist of Europe? That, I take it, is joy.

SCHWEITZER [*after reflection*]: I can answer. Yes, that is joy. [*With a forced smile.*] I would add, however, it is hardly the nurse's rôle to open up old wounds.

MARIE [*bowing her head*]: I'm sorry . . . but don't expect me to spare you. Those gravely wounded, when by themselves, will say——

SCHWEITZER [*interrupting her*]: Wounded?

MARIE [*with pointed sprightliness*]: Yes, indeed. And, think of it, I have just had a proof. . . . Nothing wounds worse than proof. [*In answer to* SCHWEITZER'S *look of interrogation*] We live but once. . . .

SCHWEITZER [*quietly*]: So I believed myself—till that little girl was born to me.

MARIE [*violently and without listening*]: We live but once! I knew it already, of course! The day a mother dies, the child is aware he is an orphan. It is only the next morning he fully understands. We live but once. My days for living are over. The cancer of time is in me. That watch on my wrist keeps time with my own pulse-beat.

SCHWEITZER [*gently*]: We live but once and yet you actually ask if you are not—just wasting your life here.

MARIE: If I am not, it is simply. . . .

SCHWEITZER: Well then, you may rest assured. It is only the people able to ask that question who will not waste their lives.

MARIE: No! Who would be capable of not wasting their lives? [*In a dull voice*] Oh, I shall never forgive myself. . . .

SCHWEITZER [*breaking in*]: Then God will forgive you. . . . [*Changing his tone.*] Look, come and see why I spilled my fruit juice.

MARIE [*going to look*]: How horrible! [*She shudders.*] Red ants!

SCHWEITZER [*smiling*]: Those are my cows at the drinking-trough. From far away in the forest, they smelt the sugar and now are coming along in perfect order.

MARIE: It is terrifying!

SCHWEITZER: Or magnificent, or grotesque—there they march, like an army—a procession . . . a matter of taste . . . but, in any case, not horrible . . . nothing that lives is horrible . . . only death . . . the death of others. [*Silence.*] So that's that. The few drops of juice have been sucked up, my ants are going back. I much prefer that to seeing them advance in procession upon the hen-house, and block up our hens' nostrils and beaks to choke and devour them in a few moments. About three nights every year they give us that warning.

MARIE [*under her breath*]: This country is too inhuman.

SCHWEITZER: It is the realm of Damocles. Death always on your track, suspended over you everywhere. In some organisms it acts as a poison, in others an antidote. [*Suddenly standing still.*] Hear that? Someone is coming this way. [MARIE *fidgets.*] Don't be afraid! I told you—the dangerous things are those you don't hear.

MARIE: But I didn't hear anything.

SCHWEITZER: Besides, Baloua la, we must love the unexpected beforehand. . . . One day, a face will appear in a doorway, you will come by chance on some book or hear an unknown voice, and at a single stroke, your life will have found its meaning.

MARIE: What an idea! A life worth while owes nothing to chance.

SCHWEITZER: Every great life springs from seizing a great opportunity.

This costume for Edgar in *King Lear* was designed by Roger Furse for Sir Laurence Olivier's Old Vic production.

The spirit of Spain is captured in Abd el Kader Farrah's costume for Calderon's *Alcade de Zalaméa*, presented by the French Eastern Dramatic Centre.

A perennial success on both sides of the Atlantic. In this scene from the first production of Sandy Wilson's *The Boy Friend*, presented by the Players' Theatre, London, Lord Brockhurst, played by John Rutland, flirts with two of the girls from Madame Dubonnet's finishing school near Nice.

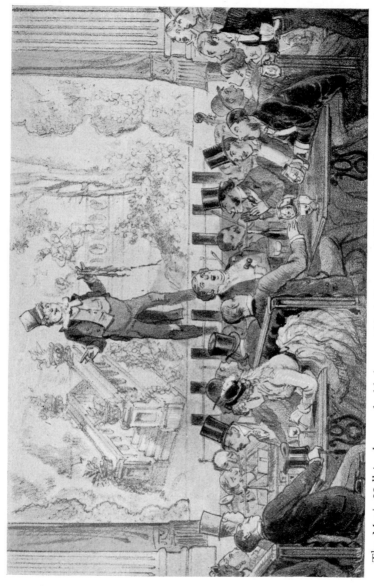

The Music Hall in the good old days. Alfred Concanen's lithography, dating about 1875, gives an idea of the atmosphere.

A Future for British Musicals

*

by Sandy Wilson

IT IS DIFFICULT to write about the English musical
theatre for one simple reason. Nowadays it scarcely
exists. There have been vague murmurs of the resurgence
of the British musical comedy, but there has been little
evidence to support them. The only two modern British
musicals to succeed recently were *Wedding in Paris* and
Salad Days. The former had a libretto by an American and
a score by an Austrian; it took place entirely in Canada and
France and it owed its success not to any of these facts but
to its stars, Evelyn Laye and Anton Walbrook. *Salad Days*,
on the other hand, boasted no stars and succeeded entirely
on the strength of its words and music and the enthusiasm
of a young company who were not only unknown to the
public but had no experience of musical theatre. But to
call it a musical play, in the accepted sense of the term, is
misleading; it is rather a revue whose items are linked by
an imaginative notion—a piano which sets everyone dancing.
So neither of these shows really deserves that legendary
title, 'the answer to the American musicals'. I am dis-
counting my own show *The Boy Friend* because it is entirely
a period piece, which lays no claim to being the English
Oklahoma or anything of the sort. It has succeeded in New
York for the same reason that it was successful in London;
it evokes a period for which there is currently a powerful
nostalgia. It is not competing with the American musical,
which is written in an entirely modern idiom. Until a
corresponding idiom can be found for an English show
which also succeeds in New York for no other reason than

that it is a good musical, the English musical must remain a poor, indeed destitute relation of its American cousin.

The reasons for this state of affairs are not hard to find. In the first place there are apparently almost no composers of original talent in the English theatre today. Our only theatrical composer of any note or international standing, Noël Coward, has only once attempted a modern musical, *Ace of Clubs*, and then with very moderate success. His last offering, *After the Ball*, was a period operetta of alarming insipidity, which came as a shock from a man who is ostensibly *au fait* with all the modern trends. Almost every other composer working in the theatre at the moment seems content to derive his inspiration quite unashamedly from America or to retreat to his childhood recollections of Gilbert and Sullivan or Edward German. There are only two composers, Donald Swann and Geoffrey Wright, who show a real originality in their work, but, both being highly skilled musicians, they tend to obscure their melodic gifts with their own virtuosity. No musical can succeed unless it possesses, quite simply, good tunes; and these British composers have been notably unsuccessful in providing.

But the fault does not lie entirely with the writers. The success of most American musicals has originated in the fact that someone with the means of producing a musical has presented an idea to his chosen writers, director, choreographer and designer and has encouraged them to create a show in concert. This was the method employed in *Oklahoma* and it is the only way a competent, let alone successful, musical can be devised. The musical is the result of an agglomeration of talents which must be moulded together from the start, not added one after another as the necessity arises. Only one or two English theatrical managements seem to realize this, and none of them seems eager to present an idea to the available talent in order to encourage the creation of an original English musical.

Most of the American musical successes have been adaptations—of a play, a book, or occasionally a film. These originals, such as *Anna and the King of Siam* (*The King and I*), *My Sister Eileen* (*Wonderful Town*) or *Liliom* (*Carousel*) are valuable properties, the rights to which can only be acquired by a theatrical management with financial resources.

It is almost useless for the individual author to attempt to acquire them on his own in the hope that a management will present his resultant adaptation. There are numerous originals in existence which could, and should, be adapted by English writers for the English stage; but, apart from Emile Littler, whose choices are not always felicitous, vide *Happy Holiday*, no English management seems anxious to acquire them for musical adaptation. That essentially English play, *Pygmalion*, has been turned into a musical by the American authors of *Paint your Wagon* to appear on Broadway under the title of *Lady Liza*—a monument to lack of enterprise on this side of the Atlantic.

It has been said in the past that London's failure to compete with Broadway in the musical field was also due to lack of talent among singers and dancers in this country. That may have been true at one time, but now it is a patently artificial excuse. The standard of performance in English musicals has risen remarkably in the past few years, and for this we must thank the American invasion. There are hundreds of extremely efficient young dancers and singers on the London stage today, and among them are almost certainly future musical stars, if only someone will give them the opportunity. The advent of Jean Carson was hailed like a second coming, but such discoveries need not be so remarkably rare. We already have another leading lady of great charm and brilliance, Sally Ann Howes, whom we are in danger of losing to America. And Julie Andrews, star of *The Boy Friend* in New York, had been available for at least five years before Vida Hope gave her the part of Polly Browne.

But at present there is in England no nursery for up-and-coming musical talent, as exists on Broadway and in Hollywood, where a score or more musicals are mounted regularly every year, providing experience and opportunity for a much greater number of artists than are ever in employment here. The same conditions apply to the writers, composers and directors. All creative artists can only thrive on work, and at present in this country the work is not forthcoming.

It is strange to think that the musical comedy was an English invention and that, for some years, America imported our product with great success. The tide has been in reverse for several decades and still shows only a very faint sign of changing. However, Broadway is a distant goal and one would be happy enough to see a native musical flourishing on our own soil, reflecting our own ideas and singing our own melodies. Let us hope that before long it will come to pass.

Music Hall—the Memory Lingers On

*

by John Shand

IN THE LAST century the music hall was the popular form of theatrical entertainment. Its zenith was perhaps reached when it was really a music hall, when the performance was composed almost entirely of songs, serious or comic. Such an entertainment seemed natural enough in days when Englishmen were more used to sing as they drank, indeed when they did not expect to get drunk without a song or two. Today, with our glasses hedged around with taxes and with laws, we must realize that the music hall, which grew out of tavern entertainment, is not likely to revive. It belonged to an age that ended perhaps not so long ago but between which and the present day there is a barrier of change which cannot be surmounted.

If this is true attempts by the B.B.C. and by theatre managers to recapture the flavour of the old music hall cannot possibly succeed. The notion is as misguided as that of people who propose rebuilding an Elizabethan theatre on Bankside in the belief that not only could one thus revive an interest in the Elizabethan dramatists but positively reproduce the atmosphere of an Elizabethan performance. Certainly, it seemed at once ludicrous and pathetic when a London theatre some years ago tried to turn itself into an 'old time' music hall by substituting gas lighting for electricity, by fetching some of its audience in hansom cabs, and by putting on the stage a number of aged artists who once were able to please. It seems equally misguided and unkind when radio producers attempt the same kind of masquerade and bring out some old stars on their last notes or some youngsters to imitate what they have never known and could not copy if they had. Sound radio and television producers are better advised to stick to their own version of what a music hall entertainment should be. They must please a vast mixed audience sitting at home.

One mentions the radio's music hall programmes because for some years now they have provided, first (and still) on sound and second on television, variety entertainments for a very large number of people which are, I believe, amongst the most popular items broadcast. To my taste they are on the whole devoid of lively humour and are at times perfectly insipid. The comedians are mostly on their best behaviour; their songs and patter seem conscientiously low, utterly for the people without being of the people; and the studio audience, so genteel, so obligingly ready to laugh and to applaud, is a comedy in itself when contrasted with the audiences in the nineteenth-century music hall, where the unoffending orchestra was sometimes caged in to protect it from bottles that might fall short of the target: the target, of course, being the artists who did not please.

Perhaps the reader may be inclined to doubt whether such rough and rowdy audiences existed in recent times? I remember during one of my last talks with Sir Oswald Stoll, the builder of the London Coliseum, he told me many tales of rowdy audiences when he opened the Cardiff Empire in 1889. One night he only succeeded in quelling a riot by walking down to the footlights carrying a fire-hose which he threatened to use if the audience would not behave. In a way Sir Oswald may be said to have succeeded as a music hall manager (and at the same time helped to kill the old music hall) by carrying that fire-hose about with him for the rest of his life. For he always disliked the raffish air and the rough patrons of the early music hall, and he set out to attract the family to his theatres. He decided that respectability and comfort would best pay dividends. He was in fact the first important music hall manager to sense what was really a coming change in social manners, and other managers had soon to follow his lead. He censored his artists as strictly as any watch committee. There was a list of 'dont's' in every dressing room and those who broke his regulations deliberately were not engaged again. 'Vulgarity' was taboo in all his theatres, and he was hailed for his courage in making the music hall fit for maiden aunts to sit in.

But when middle-class decorum began to cast its pale shadow on an art born in the saltier air of the street and the public house, the health and vigour belonging to a truly popular art began to decline. This did not matter to Stoll. The old music hall was dead, long live the new. The middle classes began to queue up at the box office and brought far more money in than had ever been brought before. Yet from that moment, an inevitable moment, the music hall was in decay. With money pouring in the sharks began to scent profits and financial considerations began to turn the popular stage into an important industry. Syndicates bought up the old halls all over the country and rebuilt them lavishly as 'palaces of variety'. Auditoriums were continually enlarged, the old intimacy was destroyed. The enthusiastic founder members of the music hall were removed to pits and galleries so distant from the stage that from them the artists looked like puppets, the expressive grimace could hardly be seen. And of course the masculine flavour of the tavern from which the entertainment grew vanished with the growing luxury of theatres built by gentlemen who, like the later builders of the picture palace, knew better how to provide patrons with comfortable seats and lavishly decorated interiors than to foster the art for which these theatres were an unnecessarily expensive setting. All this luxury had to be paid for, as had the dividends of the shareholders, the soaring salaries of the administrators and of the popular favourites whose services were fiercely competed for. In due course the local managers who knew what their local patrons liked best, and who, as their living depended on it, were sharp to notice promising newcomers and to hook them with a contract, were replaced by salaried officials who did what their London bosses told them to do and had as little say in making up their own programme as the bill-stickers.

All sides of the music hall were gradually affected by this 'big business' atmosphere. To increase profits and at the same time to keep admission prices down the twice-nightly performance was invented. Twice-nightly performances forced the management to keep to a strict time-table. Transatlantic ideas of speed and snap were introduced. The old music hall artist, like the old music hall programme, was allotted a generous portion of time. He was given an opportunity to come to friendly terms with his audience and to show versatility. If the artist pleased more on Tuesday than on Monday he would get a nod from the 'wings' and sing an extra song or so; and the audience, knowing that if they wanted an encore they could have it, were not afraid to ask for more. One encore begets another, not only for one performer but for others in the bill. A pleased audience is more ready to be pleased again. In that way a warm feeling of reciprocal enjoyment gave a keener edge to the performance. But, with the twice-nightly system and the snappier stage management it required, the artist's time was not only considerably reduced but, a more important consideration, the artist's time ceased to be elastic. When a second audience is waiting to enter the auditorium, the first audience must be cleared out at a fixed time. Encores, except encores allowed for, by highly paid stars, had to be firmly discouraged. Spontaneous applause was suppressed by a quick dropping of the curtain if, in the case of a minor performer, it was not allowed for in the time schedule.

Even the song writers were injured by this change. It is

sometimes asked why there are so few popular songs that last like the best of the old ones, many of which are still remembered and enjoyed, while even the good new ones die quickly. One reason is, of course, that the constant repetition of a song on radio and gramophone soon makes its audience heartily tired of it. But before the days of the radio and gramophone, the trustification of the music hall business destroyed, amongst other good things, the old intimate relation between the composers of songs and the performers. Publishing companies offered for songs that seemed likely to be popular a large sum down and royalties as well, a total reward that was far bigger than the individual performer, who was the original buyer, could pay. It followed that the men who used to study the voices and mannerisms of particular artists and to write songs for them, and to whom they sold the performing rights for a few guineas, now wrote for the publishers songs that might appeal to everyone when sung by anyone. The publishers did not care who sang their songs as long as they were sung as often as possible. The 'free song' thus came about. It meant that a song could be sung by anyone willing to sing it and this ended in popular artists and popular bands being offered large fees (in English, bribed) to sing or play only the songs of particular publishers. The publisher made his profit by selling the printed copies of a song to the public. That the result of this constant repetition, known to the trade as 'plugging', was to kill a song did not worry the publishers. When the artist used to buy a song he bought it because it suited his style. And because it was his no other artist could sing it however popular it became. Those who wanted to hear it had to pay to see the artist. Thus a first-rate song became part of an artist's good will on which he could trade for years. Charles Coburn's *Two Lovely Black Eyes* was a case in point.

With these things in mind one might still agree that the novelty and cheapness of the cinema followed by the sound radio and then television would have killed the music hall

N

anyway. But the seeds of decay were already in it, and the arrival of mechanical entertainment only completed more speedily a collapse that had become inevitable. It was Hazlitt, I fancy, who remarked that the main source of all comic writing is the distinguishing speech and particular manners and dress of classes and vocations. Decidedly, a main source of the virtues and vices of the old music hall performers, such as Marie Lloyd, was the rich idiosyncrasies, the vitality, the unashamed vulgarity of the populace, to which both entertainers and entertained belonged. It was chiefly to the thoughts and passions and humours of the poor that the songs and patter were attuned, to the tragedies and comedies of the struggle for money and happiness that the artists addressed themselves in gay moods or sad.

There was a common philosophy behind those who wrote, sang and listened to these songs. There was a union of feeling and experience that was bound to create popular delight. Moreover, words and tunes were not only of the people, they were of the English people. No hint of the sophisticated internationalism and the jungle rhythms of Hollywood had then crept in. The miner dreamt of home; the Cockney boasted of the Old Kent Road. The audiences knew what they liked and gave a heady welcome to their favourites; and those who failed were left in no doubt. It was a hard school. It was wide open to those who wanted to try, but the weeding was swift and severe. To be shouted off the stage or coughed off by a dissatisfied music hall audience was not a pleasant experience. But the reward of not being shouted off was the chance of being shouted for. And whoever has felt the intense excitement of holding the attention of such a crowd would not give a brass farthing for the tepid applause of a polite audience. There are a few performers today who could have tamed the audiences of yesterday; and there is plenty of talent. Clever people abound, clever dancers, instrumentalists, acrobats, conjurors, animals and, lowest of all perhaps, clever mimics. Cleverest of all are the microphones that amplify the poor thin little voices that can hardly lift themselves over the footlights. The most consistently skilful artists are the acrobats, for an acrobat who is not always a good acrobat is very soon a dead acrobat.

Marius—Act IV, Scene 5

translated by Lothian Small

from the play by Marcel Pagnol

Here we smell the joie de vivre, *the spice of life, that tang of the Mediterranean, swept by the Mistral and exposed to the Midi sun, all the meridional hurly-burly which animates Marseilles and once coloured its famous water-front—destroyed in the war—which Marcel Pagnol has preserved for us in his trilogy* Marius, Fanny, *and* Caesar. *Here are characters who do not merely appear for us in any two- or three-dimensional form ; seen on the stage or screen (who will ever forget the memory of the great Raimu?) they do not act for us, they speak to us. They invite us to join them, sit with the old cronies as they sip their Pernods on the terrace and pull each other's legs as they have done for goodness knows how many years, or the young lovers—we are not, of course, so thoughtless as to intrude, rather we become part of the atmosphere, the warmth of the sultry evening is the warmth of their young blood, nor can we resist the mysterious call of the sea which proves the greater passion. This is the age-old story of the young man and the sea, Marius with the world to conquer, Marius with Fanny to love.*

[MARIUS *with his eyes blinking and hair all ruffled looks as if he had just wakened up.*

MARIUS: Good morning, Dad.

CAESAR: Morning, lad. So you're awake at last, are you?

MARIUS: Uhu. . . . What's the time?

CAESAR: Well after nine.

MARIUS: What a life! I was reading long after I got to bed. Far into the night. . . . In fact the sun was rising by the time I fell asleep.

CAESAR: I've told you dozens of times it's not good for you reading so late. You don't look yourself. White as a sheet you are and rings round your eyes. . . .

MARIUS: Really?

CAESAR: 'Really?' If I hadn't seen you coming out of your room I'd have wondered where you had been.

MARIUS: Did you call me at seven o'clock?

CAESAR: Of course I did, but would you get up! No, you went on sleeping. Your snoring could be heard down here.

MARIUS: It couldn't be.

CAESAR: Indeed! Why?

MARIUS [*embarrassed*]: Just because. . . . I never snore.

CAESAR: You were snoring so loud, my lad, it made all the customers laugh. I was going to come and waken you, but you had locked the door.

MARIUS: Had I? Oh yes, I remember now. I must have turned the key without thinking.

CAESAR: Yes, yes, without thinking. . . . All right; but come along now and have breakfast with me. Fetch your coffee yourself. The rolls are piping hot.

MARIUS: Grand!

[MARIUS *fetches a cup of steaming coffee.* CAESAR *goes to the kitchen door, opens the hatch and speaks.*

CAESAR: Felicity! Put a cutlet on for me, and then bring me that jar of anchovies with black olives. [*To* MARIUS *as he passes with his cup of coffee.*] What's wrong with those pants of yours? They look like falling down.

MARIUS: Think so?

CAESAR: Looks like it.

MARIUS: You're quite right. I must be losing weight.

CAESAR: You read too much. It's a great mistake reading all night long. If you keep on like that you'll wind up all skin and bone. And you're not wearing a belt, I notice. Why that?

MARIUS: Damn it, neither I am. I must buy one.

[*During this conversation* FELICITY *has brought in an enormous jar of anchovies, bread and a bottle of olive oil.* CAESAR *helps himself.*

CAESAR: Better take these anchovies back, Felicity. There's

always customers about who'll hog half of them. And let me have that cutlet from the kitchen.

[*She goes out. While the two men are eating* CAESAR *watches* MARIUS *with a sort of satisfied look. On the pavement terrace outside* HONORINE *can be seen opening the shellfish counter to be ready for customers.* MARIUS *looks astonished at seeing her there.*

MARIUS: Heavens! Has Honorine come back?

CAESAR: Yes, she got here by seven o'clock in a motor car. [MARIUS *looks very ill at ease. A pause while* CAESAR *watches him.*] Come off it, Marius the innocent!

MARIUS: Why do you say that to me?

CAESAR: No reason at all, Marius the innocent. You've a healthy appetite this morning.

MARIUS [*very embarrassed*]: Oh, not bad.

CAESAR: Come along, out with it! How do things stand now between you and your ex-mistress? You know . . . the one you kept on out of pure pity? The one who tried to commit suicide? You still seeing her?

MARIUS: Yes, naturally.

CAESAR: Well now, think of that, what a lady-killer you are! And what a reader too!

MARIUS: Why?

CAESAR: Nothing, innocent Marius, nothing! [*A pause.*] Ever told her you were marrying another girl?

MARIUS: Not exactly. . . . Not yet. I gave her clearly to understand, of course, that one day or another. . . .

CAESAR: Towards that person, at least, it was very decent of you . . . it is not quite so kind perhaps to Fanny.

MARIUS: Why?

CAESAR: Because you are keeping that nice girl waiting. Have you made up your mind to marry her?

MARIUS: Yes, I've made up my mind.

CAESAR: Then why not let your parents know?

MARIUS: Because there's something I don't understand, I suppose. It's Fanny who always keeps putting it off.

CAESAR: Fanny? Why?

MARIUS: I don't know. When I talk to her about it, she says we have plenty of time.

CAESAR: That seems strange!

MARIUS: Yes, it is strange. I can't make it out. Last night, for example, when I saw her. . . .

CAESAR [*feigning the greatest surprise*]: You saw her last night? Now when could that be?

MARIUS: After supper, when I went out, you remember. . . .

CAESAR: Oh? So that was your cinema?

MARIUS: Yes, we went together.

CAESAR: Oh, I see. Well then?

MARIUS: At first she kept on talking about our marriage. She had her ideas about the house and so on all cut and dried. I mean to say it was all taken for granted.

CAESAR: Something settled, so to speak.

MARIUS: Well, yes . . . and then towards the end of the evening she suddenly changed her tune and blurted out, 'I wonder if I'm not too young to marry. . . . We had better wait a while. . . . I'm not sure I love you enough,' and so on and so forth. . . .

CAESAR: She told you that after the cinema?

MARIUS: Yes, after the cinema.

CAESAR: Maybe she didn't like the film.

MARIUS: I can't make head nor tail of it. I wonder if she's not still hankering after Panisse.

CAESAR [*shrugging his shoulders*]: That poor old fogey? Not she. Think again.

MARIUS: But then why. . . .

CAESAR [*cutting in*]: 'Why?' It's all your fault, that's why.

MARIUS: My fault?

CAESAR: Look here, Marius; you don't know women very well yet. But I do, and I'm going to tell you. A woman is something with pride, something delicate. It's all very well your not saying a word, she can sense things, she can see, understand. When that youngster began talking to you last night about your marriage, she wanted to see how you would take it. And you, without even noticing just because you are in no hurry . . . well, you must have made her feel she was talking to a blank wall. After that her pride made her draw back into herself, and mumble, 'Oh! I think I'm too young' and 'we've lots of time' and all the rest of it. But I'm dead sure that if you had told her there and then that a mass would be arranged for this morning, she'd be up and in the church before the beadle arrived.

MARIUS: Maybe you are right.

CAESAR: No maybe about it. I *am* right.

MARIUS: I'll go and speak to her.

CAESAR: Do. And listen, lad . . . the very moment you see Fanny, tell her and show her you mean it. Do. And don't lose a single minute. And another thing you shouldn't forget is the Zoë story. For ever so long that girl had run as straight as a die.

MARIUS: I don't see the connexion. Besides, I don't know the story.

CAESAR: Oh! you don't know it? Well, I'll tell you. Zoë was a pretty little thing, a bit coquettish—and good reason she had—but not an evil thought in her head. She worked in the match factory . . . I can still see her passing there along the front, a decent little kid in a huge straw hat . . . the men all had their eyes on her. For she had her own kind of charm . . . and a smile for everybody. But she kept straight, a little saint. . . . And then one day she fell for a Spanish sailor . . . she believed they were going to get married . . . that he never would go to sea again . . . so they went a bit too far a bit too soon. . . . And then one fine night, it's off he went—by himself.

MARIUS: He deserted her?

CAESAR: Uhu. So, this Zoë, poor girl. [*A shrug of despair to indicate that she let herself go.*] What d'you expect? Once a man deceives them, they think we're all alike. . . . They are so disgusted they can't love any man again . . . and so they take to the streets. And once they find themselves there, they have nothing else to lose. Honour is like a match, Marius, it can only be used once.

MARIUS: Why are you telling me all that?

CAESAR [*gruffly*]: To tell you that Fanny . . . well, that girl is not to be played with. You understand?

MARIUS: Certainly. I understand.

CAESAR: Now, one thing more. Be quite clear about this, I have no doubts whatsoever about Fanny's virtue. I have seen nothing. But mark my words, if there happens to have been anything between you . . . cuddling or anything like that . . . well then, the sooner you're married the better, believe me. . . .

MARIUS: I'll go and speak with her at once.

CAESAR: That's right, go and speak to her. But remember, be as firm as you can, for . . . if you want my opinion . . . that sailor of Zoë's . . . he wasn't a man at all.

[CAESAR *gets up, closes his clasp knife, gives* MARIUS *a serious look, and makes for the kitchen door. As he is going out, he fumbles in his apron pocket, pulls out Marius's trousers' belt and, without looking at him, flings it before his eyes on to the table and goes out.*

[Copyright: Fasquelle.]

Withdrawn From
Central Saint Martins
College of Art & Design Library

X